PERFECT BABY NAMES

PERFECT BABY NAMES

Ruthie Cheung & Rosie Cole

Dedicated to my grandmother Margaret Elizabeth Cheung –
fine names for a fine lady

First published in hardback in Great Britain in 2011 by Orion,
an imprint of the Orion Publishing Group Ltd
Orion House, 5 Upper St Martin's Lane, London WC2H 9EA
An Hachette UK Company

10 9 8 7 6 5 4 3 2 1

Text copyright © Ruthie Cheung 2011
Design copyright © Orion 2011
Illustrations by Nicola Holland

A CIP catalogue record for this book is available from the British Library.

ISBN: 978-1-409-11449-9

Printed and bound in China

The Orion Publishing Group's policy is to use papers that are natural, renewable and recyclable
and made from wood grown in sustainable forests. The logging and manufacturing processes
are expected to conform to the environmental regulations of the country of origin.

www.orionbooks.co.uk

INTRODUCTION

How to choose the perfect name

*'Words have meaning
and names have power.'*

ANON

CONGRATULATIONS, YOU'RE HAVING A BABY! We know you will have so many exciting things to think about in the coming months and one of them, of course, is choosing the right name for your little one.

A name is a tremendous gift, a gift that should last a lifetime. And if the very latest research is to be believed, it is also a gift that can put a positive spin on your child's self-esteem, their perceived attractiveness and even their popularity. How can a name mean so much? It has such an influence because of the associations it unconsciously triggers in parents and in other people. For example, if you give your little girl a name like *Isabella,* which is considered to be particularly feminine, she may well develop her personality based on this strong sense of femininity, simply because the name encourages you to nurture the more feminine aspects of her personality. Naming your baby – whether the name is feminine- or masculine-sounding, trendy or inspirational, unusual or based on family tradition or indeed anything or anyone else – can have a huge influence on how others relate to him or her and, by extension, how your child views himself or herself.

Becoming a parent is an exciting, happy time and the task of naming your baby should be fun too. Sure, it's a serious, long-term decision, but there is so much enjoyment to be had with this aspect of becoming a parent.

About this book

We hope this book will play an important part in helping you choose the right name for your baby. There are countless other resources out there to help you make this important decision, and the Internet offers a bewildering range of choices, but sometimes all that information and advice can be a little overwhelming. We are hoping this concise book will be the only resource you will ever need. It lists around 5,000 perfect baby names for you to choose from, with relevant and concise information about their origins, meanings and current usage. There are also 'top ten' name lists we've pulled out for easy reference.

You may wonder how we drew up our list of 5,000 names from the thousands upon thousands of potential names out there. The answer is we trawled through research databases and selected names that we believe will stand the test of time, possess inspirational meanings and associations, are easy to pronounce and will make any child grateful and happy for your choice.

In short, if you review the helpful tips on the next page, carefully consider your options, take your time, listen to your heart and select a name from this book with love, you really can't go wrong.

Handy baby-naming tips

When choosing your baby's name you need to consider not just what the name means to you, but also what it will one day mean for your child. It might help to ask yourself some of the following questions:

Do you want to give your child a name that 'dates' it to a particular era?

Names go in and out of fashion and names that are currently very popular may be far less so in 30 years. Do you want your child to go to school with lots of other children that have the same name, or do you want your child's name to be a little more unusual?

Do you want your child's name to impart a sense of heritage or family tradition?

If you are naming a child after a family member, are you doing it out of a sense of duty? There may be pressure from family members and friends when it comes to naming your child, but never forget this important and exciting decision is absolutely yours and yours alone.

How do you think your child's name will be received by other people?

Remember, most of us, perhaps unconsciously, look for aspects of a person's personality in their name. What first inkling of their personality do you think your choice will be giving others?

Does your choice of name work with your surname?

Your surname is an important factor to consider. For example, if your last name has several syllables you may want to avoid a first name with a lot of syllables as this could end up being too much of a mouthful. The same goes for a middle name. Think about how everything goes together - it might help to try saying your child's full name out loud to hear what it sounds like.

Do you have a particular spelling or variant of a name in mind?

If you are thinking about a name that has an unusual spelling, this can be an easy way to help your child stand out. Alongside many of the names listed in this book there are a number of variant spellings of that name. However, do bear in mind that you could also be setting your child up for a lifetime of correcting the inaccurate spelling of his or her name.

Can the name you choose be shortened and do you like the contraction?

Many names can be shortened into pet names or nicknames. Make sure you consider what the name you choose could be shortened to and if you will like it. For example, *Elizabeth* often becomes *Liz*, *Lizzie* or *Beth* and *James* will often be shortened to *Jim*.

Have you thought about the initials of the name you chose?

Make sure you check to see if the initials of the name(s) you choose and your surname spell anything. If they do it is highly likely someone will pick up on it and use it as a nickname for your child, especially if it spells something funny.

Finally, and perhaps most important of all, what influence do you think your choice of name will have on your child's sense of self?

One day your child is bound to research his or her name to discover its origin and meaning. Do you think he or she will love what they read?

Enjoy choosing your baby's name

Always remember that choosing your baby's name should be a happy experience and a chance for you to verbalise your excitement and love for your new baby. We hope this book will help you with your decision as you search for the most precious gift you'll ever give to your child and wish you every happiness in your new lives together.

Ruthie & Rosie x

THE MOST POPULAR NAMES

There are lists of top ten names throughout the book but,
for ease of reference, here are the most popular baby names
that parents have chosen since 1950, listed in order of popularity.

Top Ten Names

2010	2009
GIRLS	GIRLS
Olivia	*Olivia*
Ruby	*Ruby*
Chloe	*Sophie*
Emily	*Chloe*
Sophie	*Emily*
BOYS	BOYS
Mohammed	*Jack*
Oliver	*Oliver*
Jack	*Charlie*
Harry	*Harry*
Alfie	*Alfie*

2008	2007	2006	2005
GIRLS	GIRLS	GIRLS	GIRLS
Olivia	*Grace*	*Olivia*	*Jessica*
Ruby	*Ruby*	*Grace*	*Emily*
Emily	*Olivia*	*Jessica*	*Sophie*
Grace	*Emily*	*Ruby*	*Olivia*
Jessica	*Jessica*	*Emily*	*Chloe*
BOYS	BOYS	BOYS	BOYS
Jack	*Jack*	*Jack*	*Jack*
Oliver	*Thomas*	*Thomas*	*Joshua*
Thomas	*Oliver*	*Oliver*	*Thomas*
Harry	*Joshua*	*Joshua*	*James*
Joshua	*Harry*	*Harry*	*Oliver*

2004	2003	2002	2001
GIRLS	GIRLS	GIRLS	GIRLS
Emily	*Emily*	*Chloe*	*Chloe*
Ellie	*Ellie*	*Emily*	*Emily*
Jessica	*Chloe*	*Jessica*	*Megan*
Sophie	*Jessica*	*Ellie*	*Jessica*
Chloe	*Sophie*	*Sophie*	*Sophie*
BOYS	BOYS	BOYS	BOYS
Jack	*Jack*	*Jack*	*Jack*
Joshua	*Joshua*	*Joshua*	*Thomas*
Thomas	*Thomas*	*Thomas*	*Joshua*
James	*James*	*James*	*James*
Daniel	*Daniel*	*Daniel*	*Daniel*

2000	1990	1980
GIRLS	GIRLS	GIRLS
Chloe	*Jessica*	*Jennifer*
Emily	*Ashley*	*Amanda*
Megan	*Brittany*	*Jessica*
Charlotte	*Amanda*	*Melissa*
Jessica	*Samantha*	*Sarah*
BOYS	BOYS	BOYS
Jack	*Michael*	*Michael*
Thomas	*Christopher*	*Christopher*
James	*Matthew*	*Jason*
Joshua	*Joshua*	*David*
Daniel	*Daniel*	*James*

1970	1960	1950
GIRLS	GIRLS	GIRLS
Jennifer	*Mary*	*Linda*
Lisa	*Susan*	*Mary*
Kimberly	*Linda*	*Patricia*
Michelle	*Karen*	*Barbara*
Amy	*Donna*	*Susan*
BOYS	BOYS	BOYS
Michael	*David*	*James*
James	*Michael*	*Robert*
David	*James*	*John*
John	*John*	*Michael*
Robert	*Robert*	*David*

Aaralyn

This girl's name is likely to be of English origin, although some sources say Aaralyn is an American or Native American name. The meaning is 'with song' or 'woman with song'.

Variants include: *Aaralynn, Aralen, Aralenn, Aralenne, Aralin, Aralinn, Aaralin, Aaralinne, Aralyn, Aralynn* and *Aralynne*.

Aaron

Aaron is the biblical name for the brother of *Moses*. The name is likely to be of Egyptian rather than Hebrew origin and is traditionally believed to mean 'enlightened' or 'mountain of strength'.

Variant forms include: *Aaran, Aaren, Aarin, Aaronn, Aarron, Aaryn, Aharon, Ahron* and *Aron*.

Abbas

This boy's name is of Arabic and Hebrew origin. Abbas was the Prophet *Mohammed's* uncle. Abbas has a number of meanings, generally with a regal theme, including 'stern' or 'proud king of the beasts'.

Variants include: *Ab, Abba, Abbe, Abbey, Abbie* and *Abo*.

Abdullah

This boy's name is of Arabic origin and records suggest it may date back even earlier than the emergence of Islam. The meaning is 'Allah's servant' or 'servant of God'.

Variants include: *Ab, Abdalla, Abdella, Abduallah, Abdul, Abdulah* and *Abdulla*.

Abel

This is the biblical name for the son of *Adam* and *Eve*. The origin is uncertain but it is thought to be from the Hebrew 'hebel', often interpreted as 'breath or vapour' or 'essence of life'.

The abbreviated form is *Abe*.

Abigail

The biblical name for the 'intelligent and beautiful' wife of King *David*. The name is of Hebrew origin and is often interpreted as meaning 'father of exaltation' or 'father of joy' or 'my father is joy'.

Variant forms include: *Abagail, Abagale, Abbegail, Abbegale, Abbey, Abbi, Abbie, Abbigail, Abbigale, Abbigayle, Abby, Abbygail, Abbygale, Abi, Abigale* and *Abigayle.*

Abilene

This girl's name is of Hebrew origin. The derivation of the name is based on the Hebrew name for a region of the Holy Land in early Christian times, and it means 'grass or grassy plain'.

Variant forms include: *Abalene, Abalina, Abilena* and *Abiline.*

Abraham

Abraham is the biblical name given to the founding father of the Hebrew nation. The name's meaning comes from the Hebrew translation of 'av hamon', which is said to mean 'father of many nations' or 'exalted father'.

Variant forms include: *Abe, Abram, Avram* and *Ibrahim.*

Acacia

This girl's name is translated from the Greek word for 'immortality' or 'resurrection'. The name is also associated with a flowering shrub related to the mimosa. Its use as a popular first name is a relatively modern development.

Variant forms include: *Casey, Cassie, Cassy, Kacey, Kacie, Kasey* and *Kassy.*

Ace

This boy's name may originate from the Latin for a 'one unit' Roman coin. Its meaning is 'being number one' or 'the best', possibly because the ace can have the highest value in a card deck.

Ada

The exact origin and meaning of this unisex name is uncertain, but it is thought to be of German origin from 'adal' meaning 'noble', or of African origin meaning 'oldest daughter'. It may also be a pet form of *Adele*.

Variant forms include: *Adah, Addi, Addie, Addy, Ade, Adey* and *Adie.*

Adair

The origin of this unisex name is uncertain, with some sources suggesting it is a Celtic name, meaning 'dweller by the sacred oak tree', and other sources suggesting it is of Old German origin, meaning 'wealthy spear'.

Variant forms include: *Adaire, Adare* and *Adayre.*

Adam

This biblical name is of Hebrew origin from 'adama', which translates into 'earth' and is interpreted as meaning 'human being' or 'man'. *Addison* is a medieval transferred surname and a popular modern pet form of Adam.

Adelaide

This girl's name is of Old German origin. The meaning of Adelaide is 'woman of noble estate', derived from the translation of Old German 'adal' meaning 'noble' and 'heid' meaning 'kind'. The variant *Adella* may have developed into the name *Della.*

Variant forms include: *Adela, Adele, Adelina, Adeline, Adella* and *Adelle.*

Adlai

The biblical name for the father of one of King *David*'s herdsmen. The name is derived from the Aramaic form of the Hebrew 'Adaliah' meaning 'God is just', and is also interpreted as meaning 'ornament'.

Variant forms include: *Adley* and *Atlee.*

Adonis

The boy's name Adonis is of Greek origin derived from the Phoenician 'adon' meaning 'lord'. Adonis appears in Greek mythology as a virile and immortal youth, so his name is still used today to refer to someone who is 'athletic and handsome'.

Variant forms include: *Addonia, Adohnes, Adon, Adones* and *Adonys*.

Adrian

This boy's name is derived from the Latin meaning 'man from Adria' (a port in northern Italy on the Adriatic Sea). The name became popular in the late 1980s after the success of Sue Townsend's *The Secret Diary of Adrian Mole, Aged 13 ¾* (1982) and the subsequent hilarious series of *Adrian Mole* diaries.

Variant forms include: *Ade, Adreyan, Adriano, Adrien, Adryan, Aydrean, Aydrian* and *Aydrien*.

Adrienne

This girl's name is one of several female equivalents of *Adrian*. Other feminine forms include: *Adreanna, Adriana, Adrianah, Adriane, Adrianna, Adriannah, Adrianne, Adriena, Adrienah, Adriene* and *Adrienna*.

Africa

The Scandinavian variant of the girl's name *Erika*, but it may also be a unisex name of Celtic origin meaning 'pleasant', or a name adopted by African Americans to acknowledge their ancestry to the majestic continent of Africa.

Variant forms include: *Affrica* and *Afrika*.

Agatha

This girl's name is derived from the Latinised version of the Greek name *Agathe*, which itself comes from the feminine form of 'agathos' meaning 'good' and 'brave'. A famous bearer of the name was the bestselling crime author, Agatha Christie (1890-1976).

Variant forms include: *Ag, Agata, Agathe, Aggi, Aggie* and *Aggy*.

Agnes

This girl's name is derived from the Greek 'hagnos' meaning 'pure, holy and chaste'. In Latin the name is also associated with 'agnus' meaning lamb. Notable bearers include the fourth-century virgin martyr Saint Agnes.

Variant forms include: *Aggie, Annis, Nessie* and *Nesta*.

Ahmed

This boy's name is of Arabic origin and it is derived from 'hamida' meaning 'very praiseworthy' or 'to praise'. Commonly used in the Islamic world, the name is typically associated with someone who is considered to be worthy of praise.

Variant forms include: *Achmed, Ahmad* and *Ahmet*.

Aidan

This unisex name comes from the Anglicised form of the Gaelic name *Aedan*, itself a familiar form of *Aed* which has the meaning 'fire'. Notable bearers of the name include the seventh-century Saint Aidan.

Variant forms include: *Aedan, Aiden, Aidyn, Aydan, Ayden, Eidan* and *Eiden*.

Ailsa

This girl's name is of Scottish origin. Some sources suggest it comes from the isle of Ailsa Craig, which may derive from the Old Norse 'Alfsigr' or 'elf victory'. Others suggest Ailsa is from the Gaelic 'Aillse Creag' meaning 'Elizabeth's rock', or from *Ailsie*, a Scottish pet form for *Alice*.

Ailie is a variant form.

Aine

Aine is a girl's name of Celtic and Gaelic origin. The name's meaning is 'happiness' and 'brilliance'. Although not related, the names *Anne, Anna* and *Hannah* have been used as English versions of Aine.

Ainsley

A derivative of *Ansley* or *Ainslie*. The surname of a well-established Scottish family, Ainsley is of Gaelic origin. The name's original meaning is 'at a clearing in the wood'. Traditionally a masculine name, in modern times Ainsley is also used for girls.

Variant forms include: *Ainslee, Ainsleigh, Aynslee, Aynsley* and *Aynslie*.

Aiofe

The origin of this popular girl's name in Ireland is a mix of Gaelic, Scottish and Irish. The name's general meaning is 'beautiful, radiant, joyful and happy', from the Gaelic word 'aoibh' meaning 'beauty'.

This name is sometimes used as a Gaelic form of *Eva* or *Eve.*

Aisha

Aisha is a girl's name of Arabic origin, meaning 'alive' and it may also mean 'life' in Swahili. Some might argue that Aisha is among the best names in the world because it means 'living a good and prosperous life'.

Variants include: *Aeesha, Aeisha, Aesha, Aiesha, Asha, Asia, Ayesha* and *Aysha.*

Aisling

This name is of Gaelic and Irish origin, meaning 'dream' or 'vision'. The name is unisex but it is more popular as a girl's name, perhaps because it is considered an appropriate name for a girl who will grow up to be a beautiful woman.

Variant forms include: *Aislinn, Aislyn, Aislynn, Ashling* and *Ashlynn.*

Ajax

The boy's name Ajax is of Ancient Greek origin. Associated with Ajax, the strong and courageous legendary Trojan hero, the meaning of the name is uncertain but could mean 'of the earth' or 'mourner'.

Aias is a variant form of Ajax.

Ajay

The boy's name Ajay is derived from the Sanskrit word for 'invincible' or 'one who cannot be conquered or defeated in battle'. In short, it is associated with someone who always wins. The American and English name Ajay sometimes simply arises from a combination of the initials A. + J.

Ajit is a variant of Ajay.

Akash

Akash is a boy's name with Indian and Sanskrit origins. The meaning of the name is 'space' or 'vast like the sky' and it is derived from the Sanskrit term 'akasha', the sense of higher perception in Hindu philosophy.

Akasha

A unisex variant of the name *Akash*: if pronounced with a long final 'a', the name is feminine. If pronounced with a short final 'a', the name is masculine.

Alan

This boy's name is of Celtic origin. The name's meaning is derived from the Gaelic word 'ailin' meaning 'little rock' or 'alun' meaning 'concord or harmony', but also interpreted as 'rock'.

Variants include: *Al, Alain, Alen, Allan, Allen, Alun* and *Alyn*.

Alana

This girl's name is derived from the boy's name *Alan* but is also said to mean 'one who is beautiful'. In Hawaiian the name Alana is unisex and means 'precious, awakening, light' and 'an offering'.

Variants include: *Alanna, Alannah, Alanis* and *Lana*.

Top Ten Names Beginning with A

GIRLS	BOYS
AMELIA	ALFIE
AVA	ARCHIE
AMY	ADAM
ABIGAIL	ALEXANDER
AMBER	ALEX

Alastair

Alastair is of Greek and Gaelic origin. The meaning of the name is 'defender of men'. It is an anglicised form of *Alasdair*, the Scottish form of *Alexander*.

Variant forms include: *Al, Alasdair, Alaistair, Alistair, Alistar, Alister, Ally, Allystair, Alystair* and *Alyster*.

Alban

This boy's name is of Latin origin, meaning 'from Alba' a region in the Roman Empire, or it may be derived from the Celtic word 'alp' meaning 'rock'. The name may also be derived from Albion, a poetic name for Britain or England.

Variant forms include: *Al, Albany, Albie, Albin* and *Albina,* a rare feminine form.

Albert

This boy's name is of Old German origin and means 'noble, bright and famous'. The name therefore has associations with royalty and nobility or someone who is, or who one day might become, distinguished. The feminine equivalents of the name are *Alberta, Albertina* and *Albertine.*

Variant forms include: *Al, Alberto, Albrecht, Allie, Bert* and *Bertie.*

Alden

This Old English name is thought to have originated as a surname. It means 'trustworthy friend' or 'old friend'. Alden sounds fairly similar to the more popular name *Aidan.*

Variant forms include: *Al, Aldan, Aldin, Aldwin, Aldwyn* and *Aldwynn.*

Aldis

This fairly uncommon Old English unisex name is thought to have originated as a surname. It means 'old house' or 'elder or respected one' and possibly 'battle seasoned'.

It may also be a variant form of *Aldous.*

Aldous

The origin of this boy's name is uncertain but it may be derived from the Old German 'ald' meaning 'old' or 'elder'' The name may also be a pet form of obsolete Norman names, such as *Aldebrand*.

Variant forms include: *Al, Aldis, Aldo, Aldon* and *Aldus*.

Aled

This name is of Welsh origin. The name's meaning is 'child' or 'offspring' and it shot to prominence in the 1980s with the success of Welsh boy singer Aled Jones (b.1970).

The name is most often used as a boy's name with the feminine form of the name being *Aledwen*.

Alethea

This girl's name is of Ancient Greek origin. The meaning is from the Greek 'aletheia' meaning 'truth' and 'verity'. The name first appeared among English speakers in the seventeenth century due to Puritan interest in names suggesting virtue.

Variant forms include: *Aleta, Aletea, Aletha, Alethia, Aletia, Alithea, Alithia, Althea, Letty.*

Alex

Although a shortened form of the masculine name *Alexander* and the feminine name *Alexandria*, Alex eventually became a name in its own right by the middle of the twentieth century.

The name is also encountered as: *Alec, Alek* and *Alix*.

Alexander

The boy's name Alexander is of Ancient Greek origin, from the Latin form of the Greek name *Alexandros*. The meaning of this consistently popular name is 'warrior' and 'defender of mankind'.

Variant forms include: *Alejandro, Alek, Alessandro, Alex, Alexandre, Alixandre, Xan* and *Xander* are shortened forms.

Alexandra

This girl's name is the feminine equivalent of the boy's name *Alexander*. The name became popular in the UK when the Danish Princess Alexandra (1844-1925) married the Prince of Wales in 1863 and later became Queen Alexandra.

Variant forms include: *Alessandra, Alessia, Alex, Alexa, Alexandrea, Alexandria* and *Alexandrina*.

Alexis

The origin of this unisex name, derived from the Greek 'alexios', is both English and Russian and means 'to help' or 'to protect'. The fifth-century Saint Alexis was a popular saint in Edessa, Mesopotamia.

Variant forms for girls include: *Alex, Alexa, Alexia, Alexie, Alexina, Alexisa, Alexsei* and for boys: *Alejo, Aleksei, Aleksi, Alexey, Alexi* and *Alexy*.

Alfred

This boy's name is of Old English origin from 'aelf' meaning elf and 'raed' meaning influential guidance. Famous bearers of the name include Alfred the Great, King of Wessex (849-99), and Alfred Nobel (1833-96), the founder of the Nobel Prize. *Alfreda* is the feminine equivalent of Alfred.

Variant forms include: *Al, Alf, Alfie, Alfredo, Avery, Fred, Freddie* and *Freddy*.

Algernon

The boy's name Algernon is of French origin coming from Old French 'als gernons' meaning moustache. Originally used as a nickname, it gained popularity following its use for a character in Oscar Wilde's comedy *The Importance of Being Earnest* (1895).

Ali

A traditional boy's name in the Islamic world, Ali is of Arabic origin derived from 'ali' meaning 'elevated or sublime'. Ali was the name of Muhammad's first cousin and when the famous boxer Cassius Clay (b.1942) converted to Islam he adopted the name Muhammad Ali.

Alice

The girl's name Alice is of Old German origin. It was first used as a variant of *Adelaide*, which was derived from the Old French form of the Germanic name *Adalheidis*, which itself comes from the Old German *Adalheit* meaning 'noble woman'. The name's popularity grew with the publication of Lewis Carroll's *Alice's Adventures in Wonderland* (1865).

Alicia is the Latinised variant and *Alison* is a Norman French variant of Alice.

Alice, Alicia and Alison variant forms include: *Aleceea, Alecia, Alesia, Alessia, Ali, Alicia, Alis, Alisha, Alissa, Allecia, Allie, Allison, Alys, Alyssa, Elissa, Elli, Ellie, Ellissa, Elsa, Lissa* and *Lyssa*.

Aline

The girl's name Aline is of Gaelic origin derived from 'alainn' meaning 'lovely'. In the Middle Ages Aline was a shortened form of the name *Adeline*, which itself was an adaption of *Adele* coming from German 'adal' meaning 'noble'.

Allegra

This girl's name is of Italian origin, possibly coming from the musical term 'allegro' meaning 'lively'. The British romantic poet George Byron (1788-1824) called his illegitimate daughter Allegra.

Variant forms include: *Alegra, Allegretta* and *Allie*.

Alma

The origin of the girl's name Alma is uncertain but is believed to come from a Latin word meaning 'kind'. It became popular following the Battle of Alma (1854) during the Crimean War.

Aloysius

The boy's name Aloysius (pronounced alowishus) is a Latinised variant of the name *Louis*. It was very popular in medieval Italy and remains a favoured name among Roman Catholics.

Variant forms include: *Lewis, Louis* and *Ludwig*.

Alpha

This unisex name, more commonly used as a girl's name, is of Greek origin taken from the first letter of the Greek alphabet and therefore associated with being of prime importance.

A variant form is *Alfa*.

Alphonse

The boy's name Alphonse is of French origin derived from Old German 'adal' meaning 'noble' and 'funs' meaning 'ready' or 'prompt'. The Spanish variant, used by Spanish kings, is *Alfonso*.

Althea

The girl's name Althea is of Greek origin derived from 'althein' meaning 'to heal'. The seventeenth-century poet Richard Lovelace used Althea in his poem 'To Althea, from Prison'.

Alvin

This boy's name is derived from the Old English 'aelfwine' meaning 'elf friend'. Alvin Ailey, Jr (1939-81), an American choreographer, who founded the Alvin Ailey American Dance Theater in New York, was a famous bearer of this name. Alvin shot to prominence and popularity with the success of the *Alvin and the Chipmunks* children's movie franchise (2007 and 2009).

Variant forms include: *Alva, Alvie, Alwyn, Aylwin, Elvin, Elwin, Elwyn* and *Elwynn*.

Amanda

This girl's name is of Latin origin derived from 'amanda' meaning 'lovable'. The name was popularised in the seventeenth century by poets and playwrights and was possibly influenced by *Miranda*.

Variant forms include: *Manda* and *Mandy*.

Amaryllis

The girl's name Amaryllis is of Greek origin, probably from the Greek 'amaryssein' meaning 'to sparkle'. Its popularity as a name increased when the name was also given to a flower.

Amber

This girl's name was adopted at the end of the nineteenth century when names linked to gemstones were popular, with amber being a precious gemstone, usually honey brown in colour. Amber, the word, is ultimately a derivation from the Arabic word, 'ambar'.

Ambrose

The boy's name Ambrose is of Greek origin derived from ancient Greek 'ambrosios' meaning 'immortal'. Early saints adopted this name and consequently it is still popular among Roman Catholics, particularly in Ireland.

Amelia

This girl's name is of Latin origin combining the name *Emila* (see *Emily*) and *Amalia*, and was influenced by Germanic girls' names that contained the word 'amal' meaning 'work'.

Variant forms include: *Amalia, Amelie, Amilia, Melia, Millie* and *Milly*.

Amethyst

This girl's name, like *Amber*, was derived from words linked to gemstones. Amethyst is of Greek origin meaning 'precious purple jewel' and is regarded as the birthstone for February.

Amos

The boy's name Amos is of Hebrew origin. The meaning is uncertain, commonly interpreted as 'borne by God', but it also has been interpreted as meaning 'strong' or 'courageous'. Amos was the name of a prophet in the Old Testament.

Top Ten Strong Names

These names are all associated with strength, not just on the outside but on the inside too.

GIRLS	BOYS
ANDREA	ARTHUR
BRIDGET	CALE
KARLA	PIERCE
SELA	STEELE
TRUDY	VALERIAN

Amy

This girl's name is of Old French origin derived from 'amee' meaning 'beloved', which comes from Latin 'amare' meaning 'to love'. A famous bearer of the name was Amy Johnson (1903-41), the first woman to fly solo from Britain to Australia.

Variant forms include: *Aimee, Aimi, Aimie, Aimy* and *Amey*.

Anastasia

This girl's name is of Greek origin derived from the Greek word 'anastasis' meaning 'resurrection'. Anastasia is a popular name in Russia and was the name of one of the daughters of Nicholas II (1868-1918), the last Russian czar.

Variant forms include: *Ana, Anastacia, Anastasie, Anya, Nastasia, Stace* and *Stacey*.

Anatole

This boy's name is based on the Greek word 'anatole' meaning 'sunrise', or 'east'. The valet in *Pendennis* (1848), a William Makepeace Thackeray novel, was named Anatole. The Russian variant of this name is *Anatoli*.

Andrea

The girl's name Andrea is of uncertain origin. Generally, it is thought of as the female variant of the boy's name *Andrew*, but may also have been derived from the Greek word 'andreia' meaning 'virility'.

Variant forms include: *Andi, Andie, Andreana, Andrena, Andrene, Andreya, Andriana* and *Andrina*.

Andrew

This boy's name is of Greek origin coming from 'Andreas', the New Testament Greek form of Andrew. Saint Andrew was one of the apostles in the Bible and the patron saint of Scotland, Greece and Russia. *Andreas* has become a popular variant.

Other variant forms include: *Andre, Andrei, Andrey* and *Andy*.

Andromeda

This girl's name is of Greek origin meaning 'leader'. The Andromeda Galaxy is named after the princess in Greek mythology who was chained to a rock, as a sacrifice to a sea monster, until Perseus rescued her.

Angela

This girl's name is of Greek origin derived from 'angelos' meaning 'messenger', but more generally interpreted as 'messenger of god' or 'angel'. The word angel is often used as an affectionate way to describe a lovely, kind girl.

Variant forms include: *Ange, Angel, Angele, Angelee, Angelena, Angelene, Angeli, Angelica, Angelika, Angelina, Angeline, Angelique, Angie, Angy, Anjelica, Anjelika* and *Anjelita*.

Angharad

This girl's name is of Welsh origin from the Welsh 'an' and 'car' meaning 'much loved'. The name was given a boost in popularity by Angharad Rees (b.1949), the Welsh actress, who appeared in the popular BBC drama *Poldark* (1975).

Angus

This Scottish boy's name comes from the Gaelic name *Aonghus*, the name of an ancient Celtic god who had the characteristics of humour and wisdom. The most common variant form of Angus is *Gus*.

Annabel

This girl's name is often taken as a derivation of *Anne*, but is more likely to have been developed from the French name *Amabel* that comes from Latin 'amabilis' meaning 'lovable'.

Variant forms include: *Annabella* and *Annabelle.*

Annaliese

This girl's name, in this form, is a German and Scandinavian first name created by combining *Anne* and *Liese* (a variant of *Elizabeth*). It is more commonly found as *Annalisa* among English speakers.

Anne

The girl's name Anne was derived from the Hebrew girl's name *Hanna* meaning 'grace' or 'favour'. Anne was a French first name that was adopted by the English as a variant of *Ann* in the Middle Ages and has many variants in other languages. It is also used in combination with other names.

Variant forms include: *Anna, Anneka, Annette, Anita* and *Anoushka.*

Anselm

This boy's name is of Old German origin derived from 'ans' meaning 'god' and 'helm' meaning 'helmet', and is usually interpreted as 'protected by god'. Saint Anselm, Archbishop of Canterbury in the eleventh century, was a famous bearer of this name.

Anthea

This girl's name is from the Greek adjective 'antheios', translated as 'flowery'. The name was used in Greek mythology as a title by the goddess Hera, queen of heaven and wife of Zeus.

Anthony

This boy's name may come from the Latin name '*Antonius*', a Roman family name that was possibly of Etruscan origin. The Greek name Anthony means 'flourishing', and the Latin translation means 'praiseworthy'. The name is commonly shortened to *Tony*.

Variant forms include: *Antoine, Anton, Antonio* and *Antony.*

Antoinette

This girl's name is the feminine diminutive of the French variant of *Anthony*. The meaning is 'beyond praise'. The beautiful but tragic, eighteenth-century French Queen Marie Antoinette is associated with the name.

Antonia

This girl's name is the feminine diminutive of the Latin variant of *Anthony*. The meaning is 'priceless' or 'praiseworthy' or 'beautiful'. *Toni* is a pet form of this name.

Apple

The girl's name Apple is linked with the phrase 'apple of my eye', and is also a sweet and wholesome fruit. In many religious traditions apples are a symbol of divine wisdom and guidance. In China they represent peace and apple blossom is a symbol of women's beauty.
In Norse mythology apples are a symbol of eternal youth. The name became prominent in 2004 when Oscar-winning American actress Gwyneth Paltrow (b.1972) named her daughter Apple.

April

The girl's name April is of Latin origin meaning 'to open'. It is associated with the name of the first month of spring, the time of the year associated with new beginnings, renewal and growth.

Variant forms include: *Apryl, Averil, Averill, Averyl, Avril* and *Avrill.*

Arabel

This girl's name is probably a derivation from the English name *Annabella*. It may also be of Latin origin, meaning 'prayerful' or 'invokable'. Based on this meaning, one interpretation could be 'answered prayer'.

Arabelle is a variant form.

Archibald

The boy's name Archibald comes from the Old German 'ercan', meaning 'genuine' and 'bald' meaning 'bold', and therefore is usually interpreted as someone who is 'truly brave'. The name is popular in Scotland where it is used as the English equivalent of *Gillespie*.

Variants include: *Archie* and *Archy.*

Arden

This unisex name is of Latin origin based on a place name meaning 'great forest'. Arden was the maiden name of William Shakespeare's (1564-1616) mother. It is also the name of the beautiful forest in Shakespeare's play *As You Like It* (written in 1599 or 1600).

Variant forms include: *Ardin, Ardon* and *Arrden*.

Aretha

The girl's name Aretha is of Greek origin derived from the Greek word 'arete' meaning 'excellence'. Aretha Franklin, (b.1942) the US soul singer, who has been described as 'the queen of soul', is a famous bearer of the name.

Aria

This girl's name is of Hebrew origin from the word meaning 'lioness'. It is also an Italian name from the Latin word 'aera', which is associated with music and means 'beautiful song'.

Top Ten Names Associated with Places

GIRLS	BOYS
ADELAIDE	AUSTIN
ALEXANDRIA	BRANDON
CHARLOTTE	DEVON
FLORENCE	HAMILTON
PARIS	BROOKLYN

Ariadne

This girl's name is of Greek origin possibly from the Greek word 'adnos' that means 'holy'. In Greek mythology, Ariadne was the name of the resourceful and clever daughter of the Cretan King Minos.

Variant forms include: *Ariana, Arianna* and *Arianne.*

Ariel

This unisex name is Hebrew in origin and is believed to mean 'lion or lioness of God'. The name has otherworldly connotations too. It was popularised by the mermaid character Ariel in *The Little Mermaid* (1989), the ever-popular Walt Disney animation.

Variant forms include: *Ariella* and *Arielle.*

Arlene

This girl's name may have evolved from the contracted form of the names *Charlene* and *Marlene*. It may also be a feminine form of *Arlen*, from the Irish Gaelic meaning 'pledge, promise'.

Variant forms include: *Arlan, Arlana, Arleen* and *Arline.*

Arlette

The girl's name Arlette is of ancient and uncertain origin. It is possibly of Norman French origin and a diminutive of the Germanic word 'arn' meaning 'eagle', which gives it associations with nobility, speed and skill.

Variant forms include: *Arleta* and *Arletta.*

Arnold/Arnie

This boy's name is of German origin derived from 'arn' meaning 'eagle' and 'wald' meaning 'ruler', and therefore interpreted as meaning 'eagle ruler'. Saint Arnold, who was a musician at the eighth-century court of Charlemagne, popularised the name in the Middle Ages but it died out in the fourteenth century. It became popular again in the nineteenth century. A famous bearer of the name is Arnold Schwarzenegger (b.1947), the Austrian-American bodybuilder, actor and politician.

Variant forms include: *Arn, Arnie* and *Arny.*

Arthur/Art

This boy's name is of uncertain Celtic origin possibly from the Celtic 'artos' meaning 'bear' or Irish 'art' meaning 'stone'. A famous bearer of the name was the legendary King Arthur, who, according to medieval histories and romances, led the defence of Britain against Saxon invaders in the early sixth century.

Variant forms include: *Art, Artair* and *Arturo*.

Asa

This boy's name is of Hebrew origin. Based originally on a nickname meaning 'doctor' or 'healer' and therefore may have associations with the medical profession. Asa is a common Jewish name.

Ashanti

Ashanti is a unisex name, but a more popular choice for girls. In terms of origin, Ashanti can be traced back to the Ashanti (or Asante) people of central Ghana. Centuries ago they ruled a great and powerful kingdom and today the name is still used to honour them.

Variant forms include: *Ashantay* and *Ashantee*.

Ashley

The unisex name Ashley is of Old English origin. It was originally a surname derived from Old English meaning 'ash meadow or wood'. Its use as a boy's name is probably due to the popularity of philanthropist Anthony Ashley Cooper, seventh Earl of Shaftesbury (1801-85).

Variant forms include: *Ash, Ashlee, Ashleigh, Ashlin, Ashlinn, Ashly, Ashlyn, Ashlynn* and *Lee*.

Ashton

This unisex name, although it tends to be more popular for boys, is of Old English origin and it means 'ash tree town'. The name has become increasingly popular in recent years.

Variant forms include: *Ash, Ashford* and *Aston*.

Astrid

This girl's name is of Scandinavian origin based on the Norse 'ans' meaning 'god' and 'frithr' meaning 'fair' and translated to mean 'divinely beautiful'. Its use in English may be influenced by Queen Astrid of the Belgians (1905-35).

Atalanta

This girl's name is of Greek origin based on the word 'Atalanta' meaning 'secure'. Atalanta is the name of a fierce virgin huntress from Ancient Greek mythology.

Atlanta is a variant form.

Athena

This girl's name is of Greek origin. In Greek mythology Athena was the virgin goddess of wisdom and poetry and the inventor of music, so the name's meaning is interpreted as 'wise'.

Variant forms include: *Atheena* and *Attie*.

Aubrey

This unisex name is of Old German origin from the words 'alb' meaning 'elf' and 'richi' meaning 'power', and therefore can be interpreted as 'elf ruler'. It is sometimes shortened to *Aub*.

Audley

This boy's name is of Old English origin developed from a place name of uncertain meaning. Audley Harrison (b.1971), a professional boxer who became the first British amateur fighter to win the superheavyweight division at the Olympic games in 2000.

Audrey

This girl's name is of Old English origin derived from 'aethl' meaning 'noble' and 'thryth' meaning 'strength', and interpreted as meaning 'noble strength'. Audrey Hepburn (1929-93) an iconic film actress and humanitarian was a famous bearer of this name.

Augusta

This girl's name is of Latin origin and the feminine equivalent of the boy's name *Augustus*. It means 'great' or 'magnificent'. It was introduced to Britain when King George III, a member of the German House of Hanover, gave this name to his second daughter in the eighteenth century.

Variant forms include: *Augustina, Augustine, Gus* and *Gussie*.

Aurelia

This girl's name is of Latin origin and the feminine form of the Latin family name 'Aurelius', which is derived from the word 'aurum' meaning 'gold', and often interpreted as 'golden haired'. It became popular in England from the seventeenth century onwards.

Variant forms include: *Auriel, Auriella* and *Aurielle*.

Aurora

The girl's name Aurora is of Latin origin from 'aurora' meaning 'dawn'. In Roman mythology it is the name of the goddess of dawn or sunrise. In some versions of the classic fairy tale *The Sleeping Beauty*, the princess's name is Aurora. The name is sometimes used today as an equivalent of *Dawn*.

Austin

This boy's name is a shortened version of *Augustine* (see *Augusta*), contracted by everyday speech. It was taken up in the Middle Ages and has been in popular use ever since.

Austen is a variant form.

Ava

This girl's name is of uncertain origin. It is possibly a variant of the biblical name *Eve*, but it is also linked with the Latin 'avis' meaning bird. Ava Gardner (1922-90), an American film actress, was a famous bearer of the name.

Azalea

This girl's name comes from the name of a flowering shrub that blooms in spring. The shrub was named in the eighteenth century with the feminine form of the Greek word 'azeleos' meaning dry, because it grows in dry soil. The male equivalent of the name is *Azalia*.

Azaria

This girl's name is of Hebrew origin. Originally a male biblical name *Azariah*, meaning 'helped by God', it is now most commonly used as a girl's name, perhaps because the 'a' ending makes it more acceptable for use as a girl's name.

Azure

The girl's name Azure is of Latin or Old French or Spanish origin meaning 'sky blue' or 'blue in colour', and it may be a suitable choice for blue-eyed babies.

Azura is a variant form.

Top Ten Names in 1911

BOYS	GIRLS
JOHN	MARY
WILLIAM	HELEN
JAMES	MARGARET
GEORGE	DOROTHY
ROBERT	RUTH

Bailey

This popular boy's name is of Old English origin. The meaning of the name was derived as an occupational name from 'berry clearing' and 'bailiff', or from a place name meaning 'town fortification'.

Variant forms include: *Bailee, Baileigh* and *Bayleigh.*

Baptist

The boy's name Baptist is of Greek origin from 'baptistes' meaning 'to dip'. The name has associations with John the Baptist who baptised Jesus in the River Jordan.

Variant forms include *Baptiste.*

Barack

The boy's name Barack is of Hebrew and Swahili origin meaning 'lightning; blessed'. The name has biblical associations with Barak, an Israelite general who led the Israelites to victory over a Canaanite army. The most famous bearer is Barack Obama (b.1961) who became the first African-American President of the USA in 2008.

Variant forms include: *Barak* and *Barrak.*

Barbara

The girl's name Barbara is of Greek origin from 'barbaroi' meaning 'foreign woman'. Saint Barbara was a third-century Christian saint and martyr, who in modern times has been invoked as the protector against fire and lightning.

Variant forms include: *Babs, Barbie, Barbra, Bobbi* and *Bobbie.*

Barnaby

The boy's name Barnaby is of Aramaic origin meaning 'son of consolation'. The name is a variant of *Barnabas* but established itself as the popular form in the nineteenth century.

Variant forms include: *Barney* and *Barny.*

Barry

The boy's name Barry is of uncertain origin. It is possibly from the Gaelic 'bearach' meaning 'spear' or from the Irish Barra, a shortened form of *'Fionnbarr'* meaning 'fair haired'.

Variant forms include: *Barrie, Baz* and *Bazza.*

Bartholomew

The boy's name Bartholomew is a biblical name derived from the Aramaic for 'son of *Talmai'*. Talmai is a Hebrew name meaning 'abounding in furrows'. Commonly shortened to *Bart,* which is the name of a famous cartoon character in the American animated TV sitcom *The Simpsons* (1989 – present).

Basil

This boy's name is of Greek origin from 'basileus' meaning 'king' and is commonly interpreted as meaning 'royal'. Well-known bearers of the name include the TV character Basil Fawlty in the BBC comedy series *Fawlty Towers* (1975, 1979).

Baxter

The boy's name Baxter is of Old English origin derived from an occupational surname meaning 'baker'. The name has characteristics associated with being a provider and hard-working individuals.

Variant forms include: *Bax* and *Baxley.*

Beatrice

This girl's name is of Latin origin derived from 'beatus' meaning 'happy' or 'blessed'. A notable bearer of the name is the Duke and Duchess of York's daughter Princess Beatrice (b.1988).

Variant forms include: *Bea, Beatrix, Beattie, Bee, Betrys, Trix* and *Trixie.*

Beau

This boy's name is of French origin from 'beau' meaning 'handsome'. The name is a shortened form of *Beauregard.* A famous bearer of the name is the popular US film actor Lloyd 'Beau' Bridges (b.1941).

Beckham

The boy's name Beckham is of English origin derived from a surname meaning 'beck homestead'. The name has gained recent popularity due to David Beckham (b.1975), the England football player.

Belinda

This girl's name is of uncertain origin. It is possibly from the Italian 'bella' meaning 'beautiful', or from the Old German 'lint' meaning 'snake'. A modern interpretation of the name comes from a combination of *Bella* and *Linda*.

Variant forms include: *Bel, Bindy, Linda* and *Lindy.*

Bella

This girl's name is of Italian origin from 'bella' meaning 'beautiful'. It may also have developed as a shortened form of names such as *Arabella* or *Isabella*. The name has been popularised through the character of the same name in the *Twilight* novels written by Stephenie Meyer (b.1973), first published in 2005.

Variant forms include: *Bel* and *Belle.*

Top Ten Names After Cities

GIRLS	BOYS
ADELAIDE	AUSTIN
ALEXANDRIA	BROOKLYN
FLORENCE	DEVON
PARIS	SYDNEY
VICTORIA	TROY

Benjamin

This boy's name is of Hebrew origin meaning 'son of the right hand', 'son of the south' or 'son of my old age'. Famous bearers of the name include the respected British Prime Minister Benjamin Disraeli (1804–81).

Variant forms include: *Ben, Benji, Benjie, Benjy, Bennie* and *Benny.*

Berkeley

This boy's name is of Old English origin from a place name in Gloucestershire derived from 'beorc' meaning 'birch' and 'leah' meaning 'wood'.

Variant forms include: *Barclay* and *Berkley.*

Bernadette

This girl's name is of French origin and is the feminine equivalent of *Bernard*. Saint Bernadette of Lourdes (1844–79), who had visions of the Virgin Mary, made Lourdes a place of pilgrimage, prayer and healing.

Variant forms include: *Bernadett, Bernadetta, Bernadine, Bernardette, Bernardine, Bernie* and *Berny.*

Bernard

The boy's name Bernard is of Old English or Old German origin. It comes from Old English 'beornheard' meaning brave warrior or from the Old German 'berinhard' meaning 'brave as a bear'.

Variant forms include: *Barnard, Bernardo, Bernhard, Bernie* and *Bernt.*

Bert

The boy's name Bert is of Old German origin from 'beraht' meaning 'bright or famous'. The name was developed as a shortened form of *Albert, Bertram* and *Herbert.*

Variant forms include: *Bertie* and *Burt.*

Beryl

This girl's name came from the name of a precious gem that was given as a token of good luck. It was one of many jewel names adopted as first names by English speakers in the late-nineteenth century.

Variant forms include: *Berri* and *Berry.*

Bethany

The girl's name Bethany is of Hebrew origin derived from a place name meaning 'house of figs'. Bethany is a popular Roman Catholic name due to the biblical association with Mary of Bethany. *Beth* is a shortened form.

Bethanie is a variant form.

Betsy

This girl's name developed as a shortened form of *Elizabeth*, which is derived from the Hebrew 'Elisheba' meaning 'oath of God' or 'God has sworn'. These names are all popular first names in the USA.

Variant forms include: *Betsey, Bette* and *Betty*.

Bevan

This boy's name is of Welsh origin derived from a surname meaning 'son of Evan'. A famous bearer of the surname was the British politician Aneurin Bevan (1897-1960) who was the driving force behind the creation of the National Health Service in the UK.

Variant forms include: *Bev, Beven* and *Bevin*.

Beverly

This girl's name developed as the feminine equivalent of Beverley, an English place name derived from Old English 'beofor' meaning 'beaver' and 'leac' meaning 'stream'. The name became popular due to associations with Beverly Hills in the USA.

Variant forms include: *Bev, Beverley* and *Buffy*.

Beyoncé

The girl's name Beyoncé is a contemporary invented name that has been popularised by the American rhythm and blues singer Beyoncé Knowles (b.1981).

Bianca

This girl's name is of Italian origin derived from 'bianca' meaning 'white' or 'pure'. The name appeared for characters in William Shakespeare's plays *The Taming of the Shrew* (written between 1590 and 1594) and *Othello* (c.1603).

Billy

The boy's name Billy is a variant form of *William*, which is of Old German origin meaning 'determined' or 'resolute'. The girl's name *Billie* developed as the female equivalent of Billy.

Björn

This boy's name is a Scandinavian first name coming from the Old Norse for 'bear'. Björn Borg (b.1956), a former world number one tennis player who won 11 Grand Slam singles titles, is a famous bearer of the name.

Blair

This unisex name is of Gaelic origin. The name originated from a Scottish surname that was a place name derived from the Gaelic 'blar' meaning 'field' or 'plain'.

Blake

This unisex name is of Old English origin. A common English surname derived from either 'blaec' meaning 'black' or 'blac' meaning 'pale', and given as a nickname to people with fair hair and dark complexions.

Bluebell

The girl's name Bluebell originates from the name of the beautiful bluebell flower. Geri Halliwell (b.1972), a member of the Spice Girls pop group, named her daughter Bluebell.

Blythe

This girl's name is of Old English origin derived from 'blithe' meaning 'joyous' and is consequently associated with people who have a happy light-hearted character.

Bobbie

This girl's name is an abbreviated form of *Roberta*, the feminine equivalent of *Robert*. It is also considered as a shortened form of *Barbara*.
   Bobbi is a popular variant form.

Bobby

This boy's name is an abbreviated form of *Robert*, which is of Old German origin meaning 'bright' or 'famous'. Well-known bearers of the name Bobby include the England footballers Sir Robert 'Bobby' Charlton (b.1937) and Robert 'Bobby' Moore (1941–93).
   Bob is a variant form.

Bolton

This boy's name is of Old English origin derived from 'bothel' and 'tun' meaning a 'town with a special building'.

Bond

This boy's name is of Old English origin derived from 'bunda' meaning 'peasant farmer'. Transferred use of the English surname established the name as a first name and has become synonymous with novelist Ian Fleming's (1908-64) spy character James Bond.

Bonnie

This girl's name is based on a nickname from the Scottish word 'bonnie', meaning 'attractive' or 'pretty', itself derived from the Latin word 'bonus' meaning 'good'.

Bonny is a variant form.

Boris

This boy's name is derived from the Tartar nickname 'Bogoris' meaning 'small'. It is a common Russian first name and a notable bearer was the former Russian President Boris Yeltsin (1931-2007).

Bradley

The boy's name Bradley is of Old English origin based on the transferred use of the surname, which is itself derived from places in Old English meaning 'broad wood or broad clearing'. Bradley is a popular first name in the USA.

Variant forms include: *Brad, Bradlee, Bradly* and *Lee.*

Brady

This unisex name is based on the transferred use of the Irish surname, which is derived from the Gaelic 'bragha' meaning 'large chested'.

Brandon

This boy's name is of Old English origin and means 'broom' or 'broom hill'. The Italian-American actor Marlon Brando (1924-2004) may well have influenced the adoption of the name.

Variant forms include: *Brand, Brandan, Branden, Brandin, Brandyn* and *Brennan.*

Brenda

This girl's name is of Scandinavian origin based on the Old Norse 'brandr' meaning 'sword'. The name is also often regarded as the feminine form of the Irish name *Brendan.*

A variant form is: *Bren.*

Brendan

This boy's name is of Gaelic origin from 'Breanainn' meaning 'prince'. This was the name of two sixth-century Irish saints, Brendan of Ireland 'the Voyager' and Brendan of Birr.

Variant forms include: *Brenden* and *Brendon.*

Brett

This boy's name is based on the transferred use of the English surname borne by settlers from Breton in medieval England. Brett is a popular first name in the USA.

Bret is a variant form.

Brian

This boy's name is of Gaelic origin derived from the Irish Gaelic 'brigh' meaning 'strength'. Well-known bearers of the name include the British actor Brian Blessed (b.1936) and American film director Brian de Palma (b.1940).

Variant forms include: *Brien, Bryan* and *Bryant.*

Brick

This unusual boy's name is of English origin and literally means 'brick'. It is sometimes used as a nickname for people who are strong and reliable. It is also the name of a character in Tennessee Williams' play *Cat on a Hot Tin Roof* (1955).

Bridget

This girl's name is of Gaelic origin from the Anglicised form of the Irish name *Brighid* meaning 'exalted'. Well-known bearers of the name and its variants include film actresses Brigitte Bardot (b.1934), Britt Ekland (b.1942) and Bridget Fonda (b.1964).

Variant forms include: *Biddy, Birgit, Birgitta, Birgitte, Bride, Bridey, Bridie, Brigid, Brigida, Brigit* and *Brigitta*.

Brittany

This girl's name is based on the Anglicised form of the French region Bretagne. The name *Britney* has possibly evolved from this name and has gained popularity through the US pop singer Britney Spears (b.1981).

Brontë

This girl's name is based on the transferred use of the surname Brontë, made famous by the Brontë sisters Charlotte, Emily and Anne, who wrote such well-known novels as *Jane Eyre* (1847) and *Wuthering Heights* (1847).

Bronwen

This girl's name is of Welsh origin derived from 'bron' meaning 'breast' and 'gwen' meaning 'white', and taken as meaning 'fair bosomed'. Bronwen is a popular first name in Wales.

Variant forms include: *Bronwyn* and *Bron*.

Brook

This boy's name is based on the transferred use of the English surname meaning 'dweller by a stream'. The feminine equivalent is *Brooke* borne by the US film actress Brooke Shields (b.1965).

Brooklyn

This boy's name is based on the place name Brooklyn, a district of New York City. The name was popularised when it was chosen by David Beckham (b.1975), and his wife Victoria (b.1974), the pop singer with the world-famous girl group the Spice Girls, for their son.

Bruce

This boy's name is derived from the transferred use of the Scottish surname that was taken from the French baronial name 'de Brus'. The name has gained popularity in English-speaking countries.

Bruno

This boy's name is of Old German origin derived from 'brun' meaning 'brown' and was given originally to people with brown hair, brown eyes or a swarthy complexion.

Bryony

This girl's name is derived from the name of a wild hedgerow plant. It was one of a number of names taken up by English speakers in the early twentieth century from flower names.

Briony is a variant form.

Top Ten Names Beginning with B

GIRLS	BOYS
BROOKE	BENJAMIN
BETHANY	BEN
BETH	BAILEY
BEATRICE	BRADLEY
BELLA	BILLY

Caleb

This boy's name is of Hebrew origin and means 'whole hearted and devoted'. In the Old Testament Caleb was a devoted and fearless companion to *Moses*.

Variant forms include: *Cal, Cale, Cayleb, Kaleb, Kayleb* and *Kaylob*.

Calum

This boy's name is of Latin origin and means 'dove', the symbol of gentleness. Calum was originally a popular Scottish name but has gained wider acceptance in English-speaking countries.

Variant forms include: *Cal, Caley, Callum* and *Colm*.

Calypso

This girl's name is of Greek origin and means 'she who hides' or 'one who has an air of mystery about them'. In Greek mythology Odysseus kept Calypso captive for seven years.

Variant forms include: *Calipso* and *Kalypso.*

Cameron

This unisex name (often shortened to *Cam*) is of Gaelic origin and comes from the transferred use of a Scottish surname borne by an ancient Highland clan. The name's meaning is 'crooked nose'.

Camilla

This girl's name is of Latin origin and is believed to mean 'attendant at a sacrifice'. Camilla was the name of a warrior maiden in a poem by the Ancient Roman poet Virgil.

Variant forms include: *Cam, Camille, Cammie, Millie* and *Milly.*

Campbell

This boy's name is of Gaelic origin and comes from the transferred use of a Scottish surname borne by a Highland clan. The name is derived from the Gaelic 'cam beul' meaning 'crooked mouth'.

Candice

This girl's name is of uncertain origin but is believed to be a modern variant of the name *Candace*, which was the hereditary name of a line of Ethiopian queens.

Caprice

This girl's name is of French, Latin and Italian origin. The meaning is 'impulsive and unpredictable' and 'whimsical'. It may also come from an Italian word which refers to the feeling you get when your 'hairs stand on end'.

Cara

This girl's name is of uncertain origin. Possibly from the Latin 'cara' meaning 'beloved', or from the Irish Gaelic 'cara' meaning 'friend'. The Spanish variant *Cari* means 'darling' and 'dear'.

Variant forms include: *Carina, Carita, Kara, Karina* and *Karine*.

Carl

This boy's name is of Old German origin and is derived from the German name *Karl*, which is the German version of *Charles*. Carl is a popular name in Wales.

Carla

This girl's name is the feminine form of *Carl*. A well-known bearer of the name is Carla Bruni-Sarkozy (b.1967) a French songwriter, singer and former model who married the President of France, Nicolas Sarkozy.

Carmel

This girl's name is of Hebrew origin based on a place name meaning 'vineyard' or 'garden'. It also refers to Our Lady of Carmel a title given by early Christians to the Virgin *Mary*.

Variant forms include: *Carmela, Carmelit, Carmelita, Carmella* and *Carmelle*.

Carmen

This girl's name is the Spanish form of *Carmel* often connected to the Latin word 'carmen' meaning 'song'. The name became popular following the success of Georges Bizet's opera *Carmen* (1873-4).

Carol

This girl's name is of Latin origin derived from the feminine form '*Carola*', the Latin form of *Charles*. Originally a boy's name, it did not gain common usage but its popularity as a girl's name grew, probably as a shortened form of *Caroline*.

Variant forms include: *Carey, Caro, Carole, Caroline, Carolyn, Carolyne, Carrie, Carroll, Cary* and *Caryl*.

Casey

This unisex name, albeit a more popular choice for boys, is based on the transferred use of an Irish and Gaelic surname meaning 'vigilant, alert and watchful in war'.

Cassandra

This girl's name comes from Ancient Greek mythology and is based on the name of the Trojan princess, a prophetess, whose prophecies were often correct but never believed.

Variant forms include: *Cass* and *Cassie*.

Catherine

This female name is one of the earliest recorded names in history and it means someone who is 'pure'. It probably originated from the Greek language. Catherine has remained popular throughout the centuries, with many saints and queens bearing the name, and it remains popular today. *Katherine* is a French variant of the name. *Cathy* is the shortened version and *Caitlin* (Irish form) is one of the most popular variants.

Other variant forms include: *Cassie, Catarina, Cathleen, Cathryn, Catriona, Katrina, Kay* and *Kitty*.

Cecil

This unisex name - *Cecilia* is a more common feminine form - is of Latin and ancient Welsh origin and means, 'blind' or 'sixth'. It has aristocratic associations and was often used as a name for a sixth-born child.

Variant forms include: *Cecilio, Cecilius* and *Celio.*

Cecilia

The feminine form of *Cecil,* this name originates from Latin, and can be traced back to an Ancient Roman clan name. The name also references the third-century virgin martyr Saint Cecilia, the patron saint of music.

Variant forms include: *Cecily, Celia, Cicely, Cilla* and *Sheila.*

Cedric

This masculine name originates from the Welsh and means 'war leader' or 'kind and loved'. The name's boyish image may derive from the boy hero - Cedric, Lord Fauntleroy - in Frances Hodgson Burnett's novel, *Little Lord Fauntleroy* (1886).

Variant forms include: *Cedro, Rick* and *Ricky.*

Celeste

Although a unisex name, Celeste tends to be used for girls due to its associations with beauty. It originates from Latin and means 'heavenly' or 'belonging to the sky'. The name was popular with early Christians.

Variant forms include: *Celia, Celina* and *Tina.*

Celia

Of Latin origin, and traceable to the Ancient Roman clan name - Caelius - possibly meaning 'heavenly', this girl's name is sometimes used as a shortened form of *Cecilia.* Seldom used by English speakers until it was popularised by a character in Shakespeare's *As You Like It* (*c.*1599).

Variant forms include: *Ceil, Cele* and *Celie.*

Ceri

This unisex name is of Welsh origin and means 'beloved'. It is probably a shortened form of *Ceridwen,* the name of the Celtic goddess of poetic inspiration, meaning 'fair, blessed'. Ceri is often pronounced as *Kerry.*

Chad

This boy's name is of Old English and Germanic origin and means, 'someone who is warlike and fierce' or 'battle warrior'. Chad is also an English form of the English and French *Charles*.

Variant forms include: *Chadd* and *Chadwick*.

Chantal

This feminine name originates from Old French and either means 'stone' or 'to chant', or 'to sing' in English. *Chantelle* is a very popular English version of the name.

Other variants include: *Chante* and *Shantelle*.

Charlene

The female version of the boy's name *Charles*, but it also has associations with *Caroline* and *Charlotte*. It was promoted by the character Charlene played by Kylie Minogue in the long-running Australian TV soap opera *Neighbours*, first broadcast in 1985.

Variant forms include: *Charlaine, Charleen, Charleene* and *Sharline*.

Top Ten Names Inspired by Brilliant Leaders

GIRLS	BOYS
ELIZABETH	BARACK
VICTORIA	NELSON
CATHERINE	WINSTON
ROSA	ALEXANDER
JOAN	HENRY

Charles

Favoured among European and British royalty, including Prince Charles (b.1948), Prince of Wales. The origin of this boy's name is from Old German meaning 'one who is manly and strong' or 'a free man'.

Popular variants include: *Carl, Carlos, Cary, Chad, Charlie, Charlton, Chaz, Chip, Chuck* and *Karl*.

Charlotte

This girl's name originates from the Old French language and generally means 'one who is little and feminine'. It was made popular in nineteenth-century England by Queen Charlotte (1744–1818), the wife of George III.

Variant forms include: *Carla, Carlie, Carlotta, Charla, Charmaine, Cheryl, Lolita, Sherry* and *Sheryl*.

Charmaine

The origin of this popular girl's name is disputed and often confused with *Charmian*, which is of Greek origin meaning 'delight' and pronounced differently. Charmaine is also said to derive from the English word for 'charm'.

Variant forms include: *Sharmain, Sharmian, Sharmion* and *Sharmyn*.

Chelsea

Originating from the Old English language, this popular girl's name means 'port or chalk landing place'. It is the name of the daughter (b.1980) of the US President Bill Clinton (b.1946).

Variant forms include: *Chelsee, Chelsey, Chelsie* and *Chelsy*.

Cher

This unusual girl's name is of French and English origin and means 'beloved' or 'dear'. It is strongly associated with the flamboyant American singer and Oscar-winning actress Cher (b.1946).

Variant forms include: *Chere, Cherie, Cherise, Cherish, Cherry* and *Sherry*.

Cherie

This traditional French name for girls means 'sweetheart' or 'dear one' or 'darling'. It is often used in the phrase 'mon cherie'. *Cher* is a shortened form of the name.

Variant forms include: *Chere*, *Cheryl* and *Sherry*.

Cheryl

This feminine name originates from the English language and is a familiar form of *Charlotte* and *Cherry*. Currently enjoying a surge in popularity due to it being the name of the singer and fashion icon Cheryl Cole (b.1983).

Variant forms include: *Cherie*, *Cherilyn* and *Sheryl*.

Chiara

This unusual girl's name is of Italian origin and means 'light'. It is the name of several Italian saints. *Chiarah* is a popular Irish form of Chiara and means 'black hair'.

Variant forms include: *Ciara*, *Clara* and *Kiara*.

Chloe

Chloe is a girl's name that originates from the Greek language and means 'young, green shoot' or 'blooming'. The name appears in Ancient Greek mythology with the second-century legend of *Daphnis and Chloe*.

Variant forms include: *Cloe* and *Cloey*.

Chris

This unisex name is probably a Greek variant of *Christian*. It means 'one who is anointed' or a follower of Christ. It is a shortened form of the boy's name *Christopher* and the girl's name *Christina*.

Variant forms include: *Chriss* and *Kris*.

Christabel

Very likely of French and Latin origin, this girl's name means 'beautiful Christian'. This name is also the title of a romantic Gothic two-part poem written by Samuel Taylor Coleridge (1797, 1800) about Christabel, an innocent and pure heroine.

Variant forms include: *Christabella*, *Christabelle* and *Crystabella*.

Christian

Originally a girl's name in the Middle Ages, which later also became a boy's name – perhaps due to John Bunyan's *The Pilgrim's Progress* (1678) where the hero is called Christian – this unisex name is of Greek origin and means 'anointed' and 'follower of Christ'.

Variant forms include: *Chris, Christie, Cristian* and *Kristian.*

Christina

This girl's name is of Latin and French origin and means 'anointed' or 'Christian'. It may also be a Greek variation of the name *Kristina*, or a simplified version of *Christiana*.

Variant forms include: *Chris, Christa, Christen, Christine, Cristina, Crystal, Krista, Kristen, Kristina* and *Kristine.*

Christine

This all-time favourite girl's name is of Latin and French origin and a variant of *Christina*. It means 'anointed' or 'follower of Christ'. Traditionally, the name was given in Christ's honour.

Variations include: *Chris, Christa, Christen, Christina, Cristina, Crystal, Krista, Kristen, Kristina* and *Kristine.*

Christopher

This steadily popular boy's name originates from the Greek language and means 'carrier of Christ', or 'one who carries Christ inside him', meaning 'one who lives according to the Christian principles of love and forgiveness'. The third-century Saint Christopher is the patron saint of travellers. From the 1920s onwards, the popularity of the name was revived by A. A. Milne's *Winnie-the-Pooh* stories and their boy hero Christopher Robin Milne (1920–96).

Variant forms include: *Chris, Cristofer, Christos* and *Kris.*

Cian

This unusual boy's name is of Irish and Gaelic origin and means 'ancient and wise'. *Ciana* (variant forms *Cianna* and *Ciandra*) is probably a contemporary feminine variant of the name.

Variant forms include: *Kean, Keane* and *Kian*.

Ciara

This popular Irish girl's name means 'one with black hair'. It may also be a feminine form of the unisex Irish name *Ciaran*, also meaning 'black'. Some experts trace it back to the Italian name *Chiara*, meaning 'light' and the Spanish name, *Sierra* meaning 'saw'.

Variant forms include: *Ciarra, Ciera, Kiara* and *Searra*.

Cilla

This uncommon girl's name is a variant or nickname of two names with Latin origins: *Priscilla* and *Cecilia*. The meaning is 'ancient, respected and venerable'.

Cindy

The popular girl's name Cindy is very likely a nickname variant of other girls' names such as *Cynthia, Lucinda* and *Lucy*. It is also sometimes used as a shortened form for the fairy tale character *Cinderella*.

Variant forms include: *Cindi, Cyndee, Cyndi, Cyndie, Cyndy, Sindee, Sindie, Sindy, Syndi, Syndie* and *Syndy*.

Claire

This unisex name is of Latin and French origin and its meaning is 'bright or famous'. It is also the French form for *Clara*. Claire has remained a steadily popular first name for girls.

Variant forms include: *Chiara, Ciara, Clare, Claribel, Clarice, Clarinda, Clarrissa, Clorinda* and *Klara*.

Clara

This girl's name is of Latin origin and means 'brilliant, bright and famous'. Although once very popular it is less commonly used today and less frequently used than its variant, *Claire/Clare*.

Other variant forms include: *Clarabelle, Claribel, Clarice, Clarinda* and *Klara*.

Clare

Since the Middle Ages this girl's name has been an extremely popular English variant of the girl's name *Clara*. It is of Latin origin and is also a boy's name, or a nickname for the boy's name *Clarence*.

Clarence

This boy's name originates from the Irish language and means 'from the River Clare', or someone who lives close by this Celtic river. It is sometimes shortened to the nickname *Clare*.

Clarissa

This girl's name is of Latin origin and a variant of the rare medieval name *Clarice*. It was made famous by Samuel Richardson's tragic novel *Clarissa, or the History of a Young Lady* (1748).

Claude

This unisex name (although it is more common for boys) is of Latin origin and means 'lame'. Despite its negative connotations, it is considered elegant and is a popular name. It is also the name of the French composer Claude Debussy (1862-1918) and the French artist Claude Monet (1840-1926).

Top Ten Names in France

GIRLS	BOYS
EMMA	ENZO
LEA	MATHIS
MANON	LUCAS
CLARA	HUGO
CHLOE	MATHEO

Claudia

This girl's name is the feminine form of *Claude*. It is of Latin origin and, even though it means 'lame', it is a popular name because it is considered sophisticated.

Variant forms include: *Claudine, Claudy, Clodia* and *Klaudia*.

Clayton

This boy's name originates from the English language and means 'settlement of clay' or 'the town settled near clay'. It has been used steadily as a first name since the early nineteenth century.

Variant forms include: *Clay* and *Claybourne*.

Clement

This boy's name originates from the Latin language and means 'mild and merciful' or a 'man who gives mercy'. Not surprisingly, it is a name often borne by popes, saints and church leaders.

Variants include: *Clem, Clemens, Clemmie* and *Klemens*.

Clementine

A female variant of the boy's name *Clement*, this girl's name is of Latin and French origin and means 'merciful'. There is a well-known American Western folk ballad called 'Oh My Darling, Clementine' (*c.*1884).

Variants include: *Clem, Clemence, Clemency* and *Clementina*.

Cleopatra

This regal girl's name, which is more common in its variant form *Cleo*, is of Greek origin and means, 'father's glory'. It comes from *Kleopatra*, the name of many women in the Ptolemaic Egyptian royal family (323–30 BC).

Other variants include: *Cliona*.

Clifford

The name Clifford – commonly shortened to the boy's name or nickname *Cliff* – is of Old English origin and means 'cliff-side ford' or 'from the ford near the cliff'. Although Clifford is a unisex name, it is more commonly used for boys.

Clinton

This boy's name originates from the English language and means 'from the town near the hill' or 'settlement that is fenced'. It is commonly shortened to the boy's name or nickname *Clint*.

Cliona

This girl's name is of Irish and Gaelic origin and uncommon outside Ireland. It is a variant of the girl's name *Cleopatra* and the name of a lovely fairy princess in Irish legend.

Clive

This boy's name is of Old English origin and means 'slope, riverbank or cliff'. A famous bearer of the name was Robert Clive, an eighteenth-century British soldier and statesman who became known as Clive of India.

Variant forms include: *Cleve* and *Clyve*.

Clodagh

This uncommon girl's name, which can be shortened to *Clo*, originated as the name for a river in County Tipperary, Ireland. It is sometimes regarded as the Irish variant of the girl's name *Claudia*.

Colette

This girl's name is of French origin and means 'victory' or 'victory of the people'. A shortened version of *Nicolette*, it probably developed from the medieval name *Col* or *Colle*.

Variant forms include: *Coleta, Collet, Collete* and *Collette.*

Colin

This boy's name is of Irish, Scottish and Gaelic origin and means 'a young creature' or 'a victorious man'. From the sixteenth century onwards the name acquired a rural flavour as it was a name often given to shepherds.

Variant forms include: *Colan, Col, Cole* and *Colle.*

Coleen

This girl's name is of Gaelic origin from 'cailin' meaning 'girl'. Although the name has strong Irish connections it was rarely used in Ireland. It is now a popular first name in the USA and in the UK. Its recent popularity in the UK may be due to Coleen Rooney (b.1986), wife of England football star Wayne (b.1985).

Conan

This boy's name is of Gaelic origin from the word 'cu' meaning 'wolf'. The name was popularised by *Conan the Barbarian,* a 1930s cartoon series and film (1982).

Connor

This boy's name is of Gaelic origin derived from 'Conchobhar' meaning 'wolf lover'. A popular name in Ireland, it is rapidly gaining popularity in the rest of the English-speaking world.

Variant forms include: *Conn, Conor* and *Konnor.*

Conrad

This boy's name is of Old German origin from the word 'kuon' meaning 'bold' or 'brave ruler' and the word 'rad' meaning 'counsel'. Conrad is a popular first name in the USA.

Constance

This girl's name is of Latin origin derived from the Roman 'Constantia' meaning 'constancy'. The name is therefore often associated with characteristics of fortitude, consistency and loyalty.

Variant forms include: *Connie, Constancia* and *Constantia.*

Cora

This girl's name is of Greek origin from the Greek 'kore' meaning 'girl'. In classical mythology *Kore* was another name used by the beautiful goddess Persephone.

Variant forms include: *Coralee, Corey, Cori, Corie, Corrine* and *Kora.*

Coral

This girl's name was derived from the fashion for coral jewellery in the nineteenth century. Coral is a marine organism that grows in a variety of colours, the most popular being pink.

Variant forms include: *Coralie* and *Coralyn.*

Cordelia

This girl's name is of uncertain origin, possibly based on the Latin 'cor' meaning 'heart'. Cordelia was the name of King Lear's lovely and virtuous, but ultimately tragic daughter in William Shakespeare's tragedy *King Lear* (written between 1603 and 1606).

Variant forms include: *Cordy* and *Delia.*

Corey

This name is unisex, but it is a far more popular choice for boys. It is of English, Irish and Gaelic origin and means 'from the hollow or the churning water'.

Variant forms include: *Corie, Corrie* and *Cory*.

Cosima

The girl's name Cosima is of Ancient Greek origin and means 'beauty, harmony, universe and order'. Cosima is the feminine form of the English, German and Italian name *Cosmo*.

Variant forms include: *Cosma, Cosme* and *Kosma*.

Courtney

This unisex name is derived from the Norman baronial name for a place in northern France called 'Courtenay'. It also means 'court dweller', the name therefore has upper-class associations.

Craig

This boy's name is of Gaelic origin derived from a place name based on the Gaelic 'creag' meaning 'crag'. Originally a transferred Scottish surname, it has become a popular name across the English-speaking world.

Cruz

This boy's name – which is perhaps more common as a surname – is of Spanish and Portuguese origin, and its meaning is 'cross'. Cruz (b.2005) is the name of the third son of English football legend David Beckham (b.1975).

Crystal

This girl's name is of Greek origin derived from the Greek 'krystallos' meaning 'ice'. Crystal is a quartz gemstone that is cut to reflect brilliant light. The name also has associations with high-quality cut glass.

Variant forms include: *Christel, Chrystal, Chrystalla, Cristal, Crystel, Crystell, Krystal* and *Krystle*.

Cuba

This boy's name is based on the name of the largest island in the West Indies, which since 1959 has been a communist country. A well-known bearer of the name is the Oscar-winning, American actor Cuba Gooding, Jr (b.1968).

Cynthia

This girl's name is of Greek origin from the Greek 'Kynthia', which was a mythological name given to the huntress goddess Artemis, believed to have been born on Mount Kythnos.
  Cindy is a variant form.

Cyril

This traditional, but currently uncommon, boy's name is of Greek origin and is believed to be derived from the Greek word 'kyrios' meaning 'of the lord' or 'of the master'.

Top Ten Names Beginning with C

GIRLS	BOYS
CHLOE	CHARLES / CHARLIE
CHARLOTTE	CALLUM
CAITLIN	CONNOR
COURTNEY	CAMERON
CHERYL	COREY

Dahlia

This girl's name is of Scandinavian origin meaning 'valley'. Dahlia is also the name of the stunning and brightly coloured flower named after the Swedish botanist Anders Dahl (1751-89).

Dalia is a variant form.

Dai

This boy's name is of Celtic origin from 'dei' meaning 'to shine'. It is often used as a shortened form of *David* and is a popular name in Wales.

Daisy

This girl's name is derived from the Old English 'daegeseage' meaning 'day's eye'. The daisy flower was so named because it opens its petals at daybreak.

Dakota

This unisex tribal name is of Native American origin and means someone who is a 'friend or ally to all'. Some sources suggest that the name may also mean 'smiling forever'.

Variant forms include: *Daccota, Dakoda, Dakotah, Dekohta, Dekota* and *Dekowta*.

Dale

This unisex name is of Old English origin derived from the surname of people who lived in dales or valleys. Dale is a popular first name in the USA.

Dallas

This boy's name is of Old English origin derived from the surname of people who lived in dales. Dallas is a popular first name in the USA and is the name of a city in Texas.

Damian

This male name originates from the Greek language and means 'someone who tames or subdues others'. It is also associated with the word 'spirit'. *Damia* is the feminine form of the name.

Variant forms include: *Daemon, Daimen, Daimon, Daman, Damen, Damon, Damien, Dayman, Daymian, Daymon* and *Demyan.*

Dana

This unisex name may be an English variant of the name *Dane* and means 'a person from Denmark'. Some sources suggest that it may also be the name for an English river.

Variant forms include: *Dana, Dancia, Daney, Danie* and *Dayne.*

Daniel

This popular boy's name is of Hebrew origin and means 'God is my judge'. In the Bible the name was borne by a prophet skilled in interpreting dreams. His experiences were recorded in the Old Testament book of Daniel. The name is widely used by both Jews and Gentiles and has numerous variant forms and pet forms.

Variant forms include: *Dan, Dane, Dani, Dannie, Danny, Danyal* and *Danyel.*

Danielle

This widely used girl's name originates from the Hebrew language and means 'God is my judge'. It has many variant forms and is the female variant of the popular boy's name *Daniel.*

Variant forms include: *Danella, Dani, Dania, Daniela, Daniele, Daniella, Danna, Dannette, Danney, Danni, Danniella, Dannielle, Danny, Dany, Danya, Danyella, Danyelle, Dhanielle* and *Doneille.*

Top Ten Names in Spain

GIRLS	BOYS
LUCIA	ALEJANDRO
MARIA	DANIEL
PAULA	PABLO
LAURA	DAVID
MARTA	ADRIAN

Dante

This male name originates from the Spanish, Italian and Latin languages and means 'everlasting and enduring'. Dante Alighieri (1265-1321) is considered one of the greatest poets of all time.

Donte is a variant form.

Daphne

This girl's name originates from the Greek language and means 'laurel tree'. In Greek mythology Daphne is a nymph who transforms herself into a laurel tree to escape the attentions of Apollo.

Variant forms include: *Daffie, Daffy, Dafnie, Danfy, Daphna, Daphney* and *Daphnie.*

Darcy

This unisex name is of Irish and Gaelic origin and means 'someone who has dark features'. It is also a Norman name for someone from Arcy. Darcey Bussell (b.1969) is widely considered to be one of the greatest ballerinas of all time. Jane Austen named her proud hero Mr Darcy in her enduringly popular novel *Pride and Prejudice* (1813).

Variant forms include: *Darcie* and *Darsey.*

Darius

The boy's name Darius is of Greek and Persian origin and means 'one who is wealthy' or 'one who carefully maintains his possessions'. Darius is a popular name among African Americans.

Variant forms include: *Darias, Dario* and *Derry*.

Darlene

This girl's name originates from the English language and is a modern adaptation of the word 'darling'. It was first used and became extremely popular in the 1930s, but is less commonly used today.

Variant forms include: *Dareen, Darla, Darleen, Darlena, Darlina, Darline* and *Darlyne*.

Darren

This popular boy's name is of Irish and Gaelic origin and until the twentieth century was a surname. Its meaning is 'a great man who is a gift from God', or more simply 'great'.

Variant forms include: *Daren, Darin, Daron, Darran, Darrin, Derren, Derrin,* and *Derron*.

Daryl

This unisex name originates from the English language and means 'open', although some sources suggest it may also mean 'one who is greatly loved'. *Darryl* is more commonly used as the male form of the name.

Variant forms include: *Darel, Darille, Darrell, Darrille, Darryl* and *Darryll*.

David

This enduring popular boy's name originates from the Hebrew language and means 'the beloved one'. The name of King David is mentioned over a thousand times in the Bible.

Variants include: *Daffyd, Dafydd, Dave, Daven, Davey, Davide, Davidson, Davie, Davies, Davis, Davy, Davyd, Davydd* and *Davyn*.

Davina

This girl's name (sometimes shortened to *Vina*) is of Hebrew and Scottish origin and is the feminine version of the very popular boy's name *David*, which means 'beloved'.

Variant forms include: *Daveen, Davia, Daviana, Davianna, Davida, Davidina, Davine, Davy, Devina, Divina* and *Divinia*.

Dawn

This girl's name is of Old English origin and means 'daybreak or the first appearance of the sun'. It first appeared in the 1920s and has never really gone out of fashion.

Variant forms include: *Dawne, Dawnetta* and *Dawnyelle*.

Dean

This unisex name - although *Deana* is a far more common form for girls - originates from the Old English language and means either 'a church official' or 'from the valley'.

Variant forms include: *Deane* and *Dino*.

Deborah

The biblical girl's name Deborah is from the Hebrew language and means 'a bee'. It has numerous variant forms and common nicknames include *Deb, Debbie* and *Debo*.

Variant forms include: *Debby, Debi, Debora, Debra, Debrah, Debs* and *Dobra*.

Top Ten Names of Much-Loved Film Stars

GIRLS	BOYS
JUDY	WILL
JULIA	BRUCE
HELEN	ARNOLD
SANDRA	TOM
KEIRA	JOHNNY

Declan

This uncommon boy's name originates from the Irish language and means 'saint'. The well-known and important sixth-century Irish Saint Declán founded the monastery of Ardmore.

Deepak

This uncommon boy's name is of Sanskritt and Hindi origin. The meaning is 'small lamp'. A well-known bearer of the name is American physician and New Age author Deepak Chopra (b.1946).

Dipak is a variant form.

Deirdre

This girl's name originates from Gaelic and means 'sorrow and grief'. Despite its negative associations the name is popular because in Irish mythology Deirdre is a tragic but incredibly beautiful woman.

Variant forms include: *Deadra, Dee, DeeDee, Deedre, Diedra, Diedre, Diedrey* and *Dierdre*.

Delilah

This girl's name originates from the Hebrew language and means 'ravishing and seductive'. In the Old Testament Delilah is the woman who seduces Samson into revealing the secret of his superhuman strength.

Variant forms include: *Lila* and *Lilah*.

Demelza

The girl's name Demelza is of Cornish origin and means 'fort on a hill'. It may also be linked to the Cornish word for 'parable', and the French word 'mademoiselle' meaning 'young lady'.

Demi

This girl's name is of French and English origin and means 'half'. It is also a short form of *Demetria*, which is the feminine variant of *Demetrius*, meaning a follower of the Ancient Greek harvest goddess Demeter.

Variant forms include: *Demee, Demiana* and *Demie*.

Denholm

This uncommon boy's name is of Scottish and Old English origin and means 'piece of dry land in a valley'. A famous bearer of the name was English actor Denholm Elliot (1922-1992).

Denis

This popular boy's name is of French origin and means 'one who is a follower of Dionysius'. In Greek mythology, Dionysius was in charge of winemaking and the growth of vines in spring.

Variant forms include: *Den, Dennes, Denney, Dennie, Dennis, Denny, Dennys, Denys* and *Deon*.

Denise

This girl's name, the feminine form of *Dennis*, is of French origin and means 'one who is a follower of Dionysius'. In Greek mythology Dionysius was the god of wine.

Variant forms include: *Denese, Deney, Deni, Denice, Denisse, Denize, Dennet, Dennette, Denni, Dennie, Dennise, Denny, Denyce, Denys, Denyse, Dinnie* and *Dinny*.

Denzel

This boy's name, popular among African Americans, is of English origin and means 'from a place in Cornwall'. A famous bearer of the name is the Oscar-winning, American actor Denzel Washington (b.1954).

Variant forms include: *Denzell, Denzil, Denzill* and *Denzyl*.

Derek

The boy's name Derek is of English and Old German origin and it comes from the name *Theodoric*, which means 'power of the tribe' or 'ruler of the people'.

Variant forms include: *Darek, Dereck, Deric, Derick, Derik, Derreck, Derrik, Dirk, Dirke* and *Dyrk*.

Dermot

This boy's name is probably of Irish and Gaelic origin meaning 'a man who is free', but some sources suggest it may also mean 'free from envy' or 'free from injunction'.

Variant forms include: *Dermott* and *Diarmulid*.

Derren

Derren is a Gaelic variant of the boy's name *Darren* and means 'one who is great'. Derren Brown (b.1971) is a famous British illusionist, mentalist and sceptic.

Desmond

This boy's name is of Irish and Gaelic origin and means 'a man from South Munster' - one of the five regions of ancient Ireland. South African archbishop and activist Desmond Tutu (b.1931) is a famous bearer of the name.

Variant forms include: *Des, Desmund* and *Dezmund.*

Devon

This boy's name is of English origin and it refers to Devon, a county renowned for its beautiful countryside. It can also be a girl's name and the most common variant is *Devin*.

Variant forms include: *Deavon, Dev, Devan, Deven, Devin, Devron* and *Devyn.*

Dexter

The boy's name Dexter originates from Old English and Latin and means 'right handed' or 'using the right hand'. It may also mean 'one who is skilled' or 'fortunate'.

Variant forms include: *Dex, Dexton* and *Dexy.*

Diana

This popular girl's name is of Latin origin and means 'divine'. In Ancient Roman mythology Diana is a hunter and goddess, noted for her skill and beauty. The name will forever be associated with Diana, Princess of Wales (1961-97), often referred to as 'the people's princess'.

Variant forms include: *Deana, Deane, Deanna, Dee, DeeDee, Deeana, Deeane, Dena, Di, Diahna, Dian, Diandra, Diane, Diann, Dianna, Dyana, Dyane* and *Dyanne.*

Diego

This boy's name, which is growing in popularity, is of Spanish origin and is said to be a Hebrew variant of the name *James* meaning 'one who takes the place of'.

Dago is a variant form.

Top Ten Names of Poets

GIRLS	BOYS
EMILY	ROBERT
AMY	THOMAS
SYLVIA	DYLAN
ERICA	JOHN
ELIZABETH	EDGAR

Dolores

This girl's name is of Spanish origin and means 'sorrows'. Despite this negative association it is considered a glamorous name. It also has associations with the Virgin Mary, as one of the titles borne by her in Spain was 'Mary of the Sorrows' (Maria de los Dolores).

Variant forms include: *Dalores, Delora, Delores, Deloria, Deloris, Dolorita, Doloritas, Lola* and *Lolita*.

Dominic

This popular boy's name originates from the Latin language and simply means 'lord'. In times past, in Christian communities, it was often given to a child born on a Sunday, the Lord's day.

Variant forms include: *Dom, Domenic, Domenique, Domingo, Domini, Dominick, Dominico, Dominique, Domino, Dominy* and *Nick*.

Don

A shortened form of all boys' names that begin with Don, this name is of English origin. It may originally have been a surname, Donne, which became a first name in honour of English poet John Donne (1572-1631).

Donald

This boy's name, which is often shortened to *Don*, is of Gaelic and Spanish origin. Although it is associated with the Walt Disney cartoon character Donald Duck (created in 1934), its original meaning is 'world ruler'.

Donnell is a variant form.

Donna

This girl's name is of Italian origin and is a title of respect. It means 'lady' or 'lady of the home'. It was used by English speakers from the 1920s onwards and has remained popular ever since.

Variant forms include: *Dona, Donalie, Donella, Donelle, Donetta, Donia, Donica, Donnella, Donnelle, Donni, Donnica, Donnie, Donny, Donya* and *Ladonna*.

Donovan

The origin of this boy's name is Irish and Gaelic and means 'one who is a brown haired' or 'dark chief or ruler'. *Don, Donny* and *Van* are common nicknames.

Variant forms include: *Donavan, Donavon, Donevin, Donoven* and *Donovon*.

Dora

This girl's name, which may be a short form of *Dorothy*, is of Italian origin and means 'a gift'. *Dora the Explorer* (1999-present) is a hugely popular American animated TV series for children.

Variant forms include: *Dodi, Dodie, Dody, Dorah, Dore, Doreen, Doretta, Dorette, Doria, Dorie, Dorina, Dorinda, Dorine, Dorita* and *Dory*.

Doreen

The girl's name Doreen is most likely a variant of *Dora*, but some sources suggest it may be of Irish Gaelic origin meaning 'brooding', or of French origin meaning 'gilded'.

Variant forms include: *Dorene, Doreyn, Dorine, Dorreen* and *Doryne*.

Dorian

This unisex name is of Greek origin and means 'a descendent of Dorus' or 'from Doris', which is a place in Greece. The name is associated with Oscar Wilde's fantasy novel *The Picture of Dorian Gray* (1891).

Variant forms include: *Dore, Dorien, Dorion, Dorrian, Dorrien* and *Dorryen*.

Doris

This girl's name is of Greek origin and means 'bountiful gift' or 'from Doris', which is a place in Greece. It may also be a feminine form of *Dorian*. It is the real first name of screen legend Doris Day (b.1922).

Variant forms include: *Dori, Doria, Dorian, Dorice, Dorie, Dorita, Dorri, Dorrie, Dorris, Dorry, Dory, Dorys* and *Doryse*.

Dorothy

This girl's name is of Greek origin meaning 'gift from God'. Forever associated with the heroine of L. Frank Baum's novel *The Wonderful Wizard of Oz* (1900).

Variant forms include: *Dodie, Dody, Doe, Doll, Dolly, Dora, Doretta, Dori, Dorit, Dorita, Doritha, Dorotha, Dorothea, Dory, Dot, Dottey, Dottie, Dotty, Tea* and *Thea*.

Douglas

This boy's name is of Scottish and Gaelic origin and is associated with the name of a legendary and powerful Scottish clan. It means 'one who is from the black river'.

Variant forms include: *Doug* and *Douglass*.

Drew

This unisex name is of Welsh origin and means 'wise one'. It is also a shortened form of the boy's name *Andrew*. The name's popularity has been boosted by the actress Drew Barrymore (b.1975).

Variant forms include: *Dru* and *Drue*.

Dudley

The origin of this boy's name is Old English and means 'people's field, wood, clearing or meadow'. It may also refer to an eighth-century Anglo-Saxon Lord Dud (or Dado) who built Dudley Castle.

Dustin

This unisex name is of Old German and Old English origin and means 'dusty ground' or 'brave warrior'. The name's popularity has been boosted by the Oscar-winning, American actor Dustin Hoffman (b.1937).

Variant forms include: *Dustan, Dusten, Duston, Dusty* and *Dustyn*.

Dusty

Very likely an English variant of the name *Dustin*, this unisex name means 'from a dusty ground' or 'brave warrior'. It is associated with the English singer, Dusty Springfield (1939-99).

Variant forms include: *Dustan, Dustee, Dustie* and *Dustin*.

Dwight

The boy's name Dwight is of Flemish origin and means 'blond, white or 'fair-haired'. It is currently a popular name for boys in the USA and UK.

Dylan

This boy's name is of Welsh origin, possibly derived from the Welsh word 'dylif' meaning 'flood', and other interpretations include 'son of the sea'. The Welsh poet Dylan Thomas (1914-53) was a famous bearer of the name.

Dillon is a variant form.

Top Ten Names Beginning with D

GIRLS	BOYS
DANIELLE	DANIEL
DENISE	DAVID
DONNA	DYLAN
DIANA	DOMINIC
DESTINY	DWIGHT

Eamon

The uncommon boy's name Eamon is of Old English, Irish and Gaelic origin and is very likely an English variant of the boy's name *Edmund*. It means 'a wealthy protector'.

Variant forms include: *Aimon, Amon, Aymon, Eamann* and *Eamonn*.

Earl

The boy's name Earl is of English origin and means 'a nobleman, a warrior and a prince'. It was originally a nickname for a baron, duke or king.

Variant forms include: *Earle, Erl, Erle, Errol, Erroll* and *Erryl*.

Ebony

This unusual and descriptive girl's name is of Latin, Greek and Egyptian origin and means 'deep, beautiful, black wood'. Since the late 1960s the name has been popular among African Americans.

Variant forms include: *Eboney, Eboni, Ebonie, Ebonney, Ebonni* and *Ebonny*.

Ed

The boy's name Ed is fairly common and is a shortened form of the Old English names *Edgar, Edmund, Edward* and *Edwin*. It means 'wealthy spear, rich protector, rich friend'.

Eddie is a variant form.

Edgar

This boy's name is of Old English origin and means 'wealthy spear, wealthy protector, wealthy guard, wealthy friend'. In Anglo-Saxon England it was considered a name for royalty.

Variant forms include: *Eadgar, Ed, Eddie, Eddy, Edgard* and *Edgardo*.

Edith

This girl's name is of Old English origin and means 'fight or battle for wealth'. In Anglo-Saxon England it was a royal name. In recent years Edith has declined in popularity.

Variant forms include: *Eadith, Eda, Ede, Edee, Edi, Edie, Edita, Editha, Edithe, Ediva, Edy, Edyth, Edytha, Eidith, Eidyth* and *Eydith*.

Edmund

This boy's name is of Old English origin and means 'a wealthy protector or guard of wealth'. The French variant is *Edmond*. It was the name of a popular ninth-century East Anglian king and saint who was killed by Viking pagans for his faith.

Variant forms include: *Ed, Eddie, Eddy, Edmon, Edmonde, Edmondo* and *Edmundo*.

Edward

This boy's name is of Old English origin and means 'protector or guard of wealth'. First used in the ninth century, it has remained enduringly popular ever since.

Variant forms include: *Ed, Eddie, Eddy, Edik, Edison, Edouard, Eduard, Eduardo, Edvard, Edvardas, Edwardo, Edwards, Ewart, Ned, Neddie, Ted* and *Teddie*.

Eileen

This girl's name is very likely an Irish variant of the name *Helen*, which means 'light or lighting up the world'. Some sources suggest it may also be a variant of *Evelyn*.

Variant forms include: *Aileen, Ailene, Alene, Aline, Ayleen, Eila, Eilah, Eilean, Eileene, Eilena, Eilene, Eiley, Eilin, Eilleen, Eily, Ileana, Leana, Lena, Lianna* and *Lina*.

Elaine

The girl's name Elaine is probably of Greek origin and means 'sun, ray and bright light'. It may also be a French variant of *Helen*, which means 'shining light'.

Variant forms include: *Alaina, Alayna, Alayne, Allaine, Elaene, Elaina, Elaini, Elana, Elane, Elanna, Elayna, Elayne, Ellaine, Ellane, Ellayne, Elle, Ellie* and *Layney*.

Eleanor

The girl's name Eleanor is a variant of *Helen*. It is of Greek origin and means 'sun, ray and shining light'. Some sources suggest it may originate from a Greek word meaning 'compassion'.

Variant forms include: *El, Elaine, Eleanore, Elen, Elena, Eleni, Elenor, Elenora, Elenore, Eleonor, Eleonora, Elinor, Elinore, Ella, Ellen, Ellene, Ellenor, Ellenora, Ellenore, Elleonor, Elli, Ellie, Ellin* and *Leanora*.

Electra

This rather striking and unusual girl's name is of Greek origin and means 'radiant, shining and bright'. In Greek mythology Electra is the daughter of King Agamemnon.

Variant forms include: *Elektra, Elettra, Ellectra* and *Ellektra*.

Elga

The girl's name Elga is of Slavic origin and its meaning is 'one who is holy, blessed or sacred'. It is more commonly used in the Old Norse form, *Olga*.

Eli

This boy's name originates from the Hebrew language and means 'high' or 'with the help of God'. In the Old Testament Eli is a priest and judge who raises the prophet *Samuel*.

Variant forms include: *Eloy* and *Ely*.

Elizabeth

This girl's name originates from the Hebrew language and means 'God's promise' or 'God is my judge'. It has remained enduring popular in England since the reign of Queen Elizabeth I in the sixteenth century and has over 150 variant forms, just some of which are listed below.

Variant forms include: *Bess, Bessie, Bessy, Bet, Beta, Beth, Bethie, Betina, Betsey, Betsie, Betsy, Bett, Betta, Bette, Betti, Bettina, Bettine, Betty, Bettye, Bit, Bizzy, Buffy, Elisabet, Elisabeth, Elisabethe, Elisabetta, Elisah, Elise, Elissa, Elizabeth, Eliz, Eliza, Elizabet, Elizabett, Elizabette, Elizabiff, Elizabith, Elize, Elizebeth, Elle, Ellissa, Elliza, Ellsa, Elspet, Elspeth, Libby, Lisa, Lisabeth, Lise, Liz* and *Liza*.

Elke

The uncommon girl's name Elke is of Old German origin and means 'noble'. It is believed to be a variant of the popular girl's name *Alice*.

Variant forms include: *Elka* and *Ellke. Elkie?*

Ella

This girl's name is of Old German origin and means 'other', as in 'stranger or foreigner'. It may also mean 'goddess' in Hebrew and be a shortened form for *Alice, Eleanor* and *Ellen*.

Variant forms include: *Elle, Ellee, Ellie, Ellina* and *Elly*.

Ellen

The girl's name Ellen is of Greek origin and its meaning is 'bright one or sun, ray and shining light'. It is a popular variant of *Helen* and a pet name for *Eleanor*.

Variant forms include: *Elen, Elena, Elene, Eleni, Elin, Ellene, Ellie, Ellin, Ellon, Elly* and *Elynn*.

Ellery

This boy's name originates from Latin and means 'alder tree'. Some sources suggest it may also mean 'happy'. It became popular in the 1930s due to the American fictional detective Ellery Queen.

Variant forms include: *Ellary* and *Elrey*.

Elliot

This fairly popular boy's name derives from a surname and originates from Greek and Hebrew. The name's meaning is 'God is my witness' or 'the Lord is my God'.

Variant forms include: *Eli, Eliot, Eliott, Elliott, Elyot* and *Elyott*.

Ellis

This unisex name originates from the English language and is an Anglicisation of the Hebrew *Elijah*, meaning 'the Lord is my God'. It is more popular as a boy's name.

Variant forms include: *Elliss* and *Ellyce*.

Elsie

This girl's name, a variant form *Elsy*, is of Hebrew and Scottish origin. It is believed to be a variant form of *Elspeth* with the pet form *Elsie*, which in turn is a variant form of *Elizabeth*.

Elton

This boy's name is of Old English origin and means 'from Ella', a place in England, or 'from the old town'. Flamboyant singer Sir Elton John (b.1947) is a famous bearer of the name.

Variant forms include: *Alton* and *Ellton*.
Elvis This boy's name is likely to be of Scandinavian origin and means 'one who is wise'. It was made famous by Elvis Presley (1935-77), aka the 'King of Rock and Roll'.

Variant forms include: *Alvis, Alvys, Elviss* and *Elvys*.

Emile

This boy's name originates from the Latin language and means 'one who is industrious and eager'. The popularity of this unusual boy's name peaked in the early 1900s but has fallen since.

Emilia

This girl's name originates from the Latin language and means 'one who is hardworking and industrious'. The name is also an English variant of *Amelia* and Spanish variant of *Emily*.

Variant forms include: *Emelia, Emiliana* and *Emilyah.*

Emily

The popular girl's name Emily originates from the Latin language and means 'one who is hardworking and industrious ' and 'peaceful home'. Nineteenth-century novelist and poet Emily Brontë (1818–48) is a famous bearer of the name.

Variant forms include: *Ameilia, Amy, Emeline, Emilia* and *Emmy.*

Emlyn

This unisex name is of Welsh origin from the Welsh town of Castell Newydd Emlyn. It is also a variant of *Emily* and means 'eager and industrious'.

Emlen is a variant form.

Emma

This popular girl's name is of Old German and French origin and means 'whole, entire and universal'. Emma is the heroine of Jane Austen's ever-popular romantic novel of the same name, *Emma* (1815).

Variant forms include: *Em, Emm, Emeline, Emmeline, Emmy* and *Ima.*

Emmanuel

This unusual and striking boy's name is of Hebrew origin and means 'God is with us'. Currently rising in popularity, pet forms of the name include *Man, Manny* and *Mannie.*

Variant forms include: *Eman, Emanual, Emanuel, Immanuel* and *Manuel.*

Eric

This boy's name is of Old Norse origin and means 'one who is forever alone, ruler'. It was spelled *Erik* in its original form, a name borne by numerous Danish kings.

Variant forms include: *Erich, Erick, Eriq, Erix, Errick, Eryk, Rick* and *Rikky.*

Erica

This girl's name is the feminine form of *Eric*, which is of Old Norse origin and means 'one who is forever alone, ruler'. Erica is also the Latin name for the heather plant.

Variant forms include: *Erikka, Erricka, Eryca, Erycka, Eryka, Eyrica* and *Ricky*.

Erin

This popular unisex name is of Gaelic origin and means 'Ireland'. Erin is the poetic name often used for Ireland in ballads. Today, Erin is more typically a girl's name.

Variant forms include: *Eire, Eirin, Eirinn, Eiryn, Eirynn, Erienne, Erina, Erinn, Erinna, Erinne* and *Eryn*.

Ernest

This boy's name is of Old German origin and means 'to fight to the death'. In English it means one who is 'sincere, serious and determined to do the honest and right thing'.

Variant forms include: *Earnest, Ernesto, Ernie* and *Ernst*.

Errol

The uncommon boy's name Errol or *Erroll* is very likely an Old English variant of the boy's name *Earl*, which means 'a wandering nobleman, warrior or prince'.

Esme

Originally a boy's name, Esme is now more commonly a girl's name, and a shortened form of *Esmeralda*. It is of Old French origin and means 'esteemed or loved'.

Top Ten 'Beautiful' Names

These names mean beautiful or handsome, on the outside and the inside.

GIRLS	BOYS
AURORA	ADAM
BELLA	BEAU
DANIELLE	BLAKE
JEWEL	GRANT
KEIRA	JUDE

Esmeralda

The girl's name Esmeralda is of Spanish origin and means 'emerald'. It is the name of the gypsy girl and love interest in Victor Hugo's novel *The Hunchback of Notre-Dame* (1831).

Variant forms include: *Emerald, Esma, Esmaralda, Esmarelda, Esmie, Esmiralda, Esmiralde* and *Ezmeralda*.

Estelle

This uncommon girl's name is of Old French and Latin origin and means 'bright star'. It is a variant form of the English, Italian and German name *Stella*.

Variant forms include: *Estel, Estela, Estele* and *Stelle*.

Esther

This girl's name is of Persian origin and means 'myrtle leaf'. In the Bible Esther is a beautiful Jewish orphan who becomes the Queen of Persia and saves many Jews from death.

Variant forms include: *Essie, Ester* and *Hester*.

Ethan

The boy's name Ethan is of Hebrew origin and means 'one who is long lived and enduring'. In the Old Testament the name is borne by Ethan the Ezrahite, a man of great wisdom.

Variant forms include: *Etan* and *Ethen*.

Eugene

This boy's name is of Ancient Greek origin and means 'one who is well born or noble'. In its various forms the name has been borne by saints and popes down the centuries.

Variant forms include: *Eugen, Eugenio, Eugenios* and *Eugenius*.

Eustace

This boy's name is of Ancient Greek origin and means 'good harvest and fruitful'. Eustace may also derive from 'Eustathios', a Greek word meaning 'good grapes, to stand'.

Variant forms include: *Eustache, Eustatius, Eustazio, Eustis* and *Eustiss*.

Evan

This popular boy's name is of Welsh and Scottish origin and means 'God's grace'. In Celtic tradition the name means 'youthful warrior', and in Hebrew it means 'rock'.

Variant forms include: *Euan, Euen, Evann, Evans, Evon, Evyn, Ewan* and *Ewen*.

Evangeline

The girl's name Evangeline is of Greek origin and means 'good or happy news'. It is from 'evangel' the word for the gospels. It is often shortened to *Eva*.

Variant forms include: *Evan, Evangela, Evangelia, Evangelina, Evangelista, Evangelyn* and *Eve*.

Eve

This popular girl's name is of Hebrew origin and means 'life'. In the Old Testament book of Genesis it is the name of the first woman, created from Adam's rib.

Variant forms include: *Eva, Evaleen, Evelina, Evie* and *Evonne*.

Evelyn

The origin of this girl's name may be a variant of the Norman name *Ava* or *Aveline*. It may be from the Old German name *Avila*, meaning 'bird', or perhaps result from a combination of *Eve* and *Lynn*.

Variant forms include: *Evalyn, Evelin, Evelina, Evie, Evilyn, Evlin* and *Evlyn*.

Evie

This girl's name is a variant of the Norman *Evelyn* and the Hebrew *Eve*. It means 'life and animal' and is currently a very popular name and pet form for *Eve, Eva, Evangeline* and *Evelyn*.

Ewan

This boy's name, which is growing in popularity, is a variant of *Evan, Ewen, Euan, John* and *Owen* and means 'one who is youthful, born of yew and filled with God's grace'.

Top Ten Names Beginning with E

GIRLS	BOYS
EMILY	ETHAN
EVIE	EVAN
ELLA	EWAN
ELLIE	ELLIS
ERIN	ELLIOT

Faith

This girl's name is rare today and originates from the English language. It means 'loyalty, and constant belief', which together with *Hope* and *Charity* were names that Puritans adored.

Variant forms include: *Fae, Faithe, Fay, Faye, Fayth, Faythe* and *Fe*.

Farrah

The origin of this girl's name is both English and Persian. The English name means 'attractive and good-looking', and the Persian name means 'charisma and joy'.

Variant forms include: *Fara, Farah* and *Farra*.

Fay

This girl's name is of Old French origin. It is actually the French word for 'faith' and probably a shortened form of the name *Faith*. It is also a boy's name, but is more commonly used for girls. In Irish and Gaelic the name means 'raven'.

Variant forms include: *Fae, Fayanna, Faye, Fee* and *Fey*.

Felicity

This girl's name is of Latin origin and means 'good luck, good fortune and happiness'. Like *Faith, Grace, Hope* and *Charity*, it is a girl's name associated with virtue.

Variant forms include: *Felicita, Felicitas* and *Felicite*.

Felix

This boy's name is of Latin origin and means 'one who is fortunate, lucky, successful and happy'. The auspicious nature of the name made it a popular choice in the Middle Ages.

Variant forms include: *Felic, Felice, Felizio* and *Felyx*.

Fenella

This rare girl's name is of Irish and Gaelic origin and means 'white shoulder'. It is the Anglicised form of the Irish name *Fionnuala*. In Irish mythology Fionnuala was transformed into a swan.

Variant forms include: *Finella* and *Fynella*.

Ferdinand

This boy's name is of Old German origin and means 'bold voyager' or 'peace through bravery'. The name was used by early Spanish royalty including, in the eleventh century, Ferdinand the Great, King of Castile.

Variant forms include: *Ferd, Ferdie, Ferdinando, Ferdo, Ferdynand, Fernando, Hernando* and *Nando*.

Fergall

The boy's name Fergall is of Gaelic and Irish origin and means 'one who is manly and brave'. It is predominantly an Irish name and fairly uncommon outside Ireland today.

Variant forms include: *Fergal* and *Fearghal*.

Fergus

This boy's name is of Scottish and Irish origin and means 'first choice' or 'a superior man'. In Irish legend it was borne by the fifth-century, warrior prince, Fergus mac Erca.

Variant forms include: *Fearghas, Fearghus, Fergie, Ferguson* and *Fergusson*.

Fern

This girl's name is of Old English origin and the meaning is derived from the Old English 'fearn' meaning 'a shade-loving green plant'. Fern was adopted by English speakers in the nineteenth century, together with other flower and plant names.

Variant forms include: *Ferne* and *Ferna*.

Fernando

This boy's name is of Spanish origin and means 'adventurer'. In 1975 'Fernando' became the biggest-selling single of all time for the Swedish pop group ABBA.

Variant forms include: *Ferdinand, Fernand* and *Hernando*.

Ffion

This uncommon girl's name is an Irish variant of *Fiona* and means 'one who is fair and pale'. Some sources suggest it is a Welsh name and means 'foxglove'.

Fidel

A modern form of the Puritan boy's name *Faithful*, Fidel is of Old English origin. It is borne by the revolutionary leader Fidel Castro (b.1926), who became president of Cuba.

Variant forms include: *Fidalio, Fidele, Fidelo* and *Fido*.

Fidelia

This rare girl's name is a variant of the uncommon girl's name *Fidelity*. It is of Latin origin and means 'loyalty'. It is also a Latin form of the name *Faith*.

Fifi

The girl's name Fifi originates from the French language. It is a shortened form of *Josephine*, which in Hebrew means 'Jehovah increases'. It is the clichéd name for a French poodle.

Finlay

This popular boy's name is of Irish and Gaelic origin and means 'a brave, fair haired man'. The variant spelling *Finley* is also a popular name for boys.

Variant forms include: *Findlay, Finlea, Finlee, Finley, Finn, Finnlea* and *Finnley*.

Finn

The boy's name Finn is of Irish, Gaelic and German origin and means 'fair' or 'white'. In Irish legend, Finn mac Cumail was a third-century hero, in the vein of Robin Hood. Many say he was a giant.

Variant forms include: *Fin, Fingal* and *Fingall*.

Finola

This uncommon girl's name is of Gaelic and Irish origin and means 'white, shoulder'. Finola is a variant form of the English, Irish and Scottish name *Fenella*.

Fiona

The popular girl's name Fiona is of Gaelic and Irish origin and means 'fair and pale'. It may be the feminine equivalent of *Finn*: reportedly adopted by English speakers in the eighteenth century, due to its use by James Macpherson (1736-96) in his Ossianic poems.

Variant forms include: *Fee, Ffion, Ffiona, Ffyona, Fione, Fionna* and *Fyonadue*.

Fitzgerald

This unusual boy's name is of Old French and Old German origin and means 'son of the ruler with the spear'. It is often shortened to the pet name *Fitz*.

Fitzroy

The unusual boy's name Fitzroy is of Old French origin and means 'the son of the king'. It is often shortened to the pet name *Fitz*.

Flavia

The origin of the uncommon girl's name Flavia is Latin. It is the feminine form of a Roman clan name, Flavius, and means 'blond or yellow-haired one'.

Fletcher

The boy's name Fletcher, often shortened to its pet form *Fletch*, is of Middle English origin and is associated with an occupation. It means 'arrow maker or arrow featherer'.

Fleur

The uncommon girl's name Fleur is of French origin and means 'flower'. It was adopted by English speakers in the twentieth century, following an appearance in second book of *The Forsyte Saga - In Chancery* (1920) - by John Galsworthy.

Flint

This uncommon boy's name is of Old English origin and means 'stream' or 'one who lives near a stream'. It also refers to the quartz that produces sparks when struck with steel.

Flynt is a variant form.

Flora

The girl's name Flora is of Latin origin and means 'flower'. In Roman mythology it is the name of the Roman goddess of flowers and blossoms and springtime.

Variant forms include: *Fiora, Fleur* and *Florida.*

Florence

This girl's name is of Latin origin and means 'flowering or in bloom'. It is also the name of an Italian city, and the first name of the English nurse Florence Nightingale (1820-1910).

Variant forms include: *Flo* and *Flora.*

Floyd

The boy's name Floyd is of Welsh origin and means 'grey or grey haired'. Derived from a surname, the name has seen a dip in popularity in recent years.

Flynn

This uncommon boy's name is of Irish and Gaelic origin and means 'one with a ruddy complexion' or 'red one' or 'son of the red one'.

Variant forms include: *Flin, Flinn* and *Flyn.*

Top Ten Names After Plants

GIRLS	BOYS
HOLLY	BRIAR
DAISY	ADONIS
POPPY	HEDLEY
LILY	SHELDON
ANGELICA	HOLLIS

Forbes

The uncommon boy's name Forbes is of Irish and Gaelic origin and means 'field'. It may also mean 'owner of fields' or 'prosperous or wealthy one'.

Ford

The boy's name Ford is of Old English origin and means 'river crossing'. Many people associate it with the car of the same name. It is also a pet form of the name *Clifford*.

Variant forms include: *Forde, Forden* and *Fordon*.

Forrest

The boy's name Forrest is a variant of the Old French *Forest* and means 'woodsman'; associated with the Oscar-winning movie *Forrest Gump* (1994), starring American actor Tom Hanks (b.1956) in the title role.

Fox

This boy's name is of Old English origin and simply means 'fox', the swift and crafty mammal predator with russet-coloured hair. The name is in irregular use today.

Frances

The girl's name Frances is of Latin origin and is the feminine spelling of the boy's name *Francis*. The meaning of the name is 'woman from France, or free woman'.

Variant forms include: *Fanny, Fran, Francesca* and *Francine*.

Francesca

This girl's name is of Italian origin and a popular variant of the Latin girl's name *Frances*. Predominantly used in Italy, the name means 'Frenchwoman or free one'.

Variant forms include: *Franceska, Franchesa* and *Francisca*.

Francesco

This boy's name is of Italian origin and a variant of the boy's name *Francis*. It means 'French man or free man'. It is predominantly used by Italians.

Francis

The boy's name Francis is of Latin origin and means 'Frenchman or free man'. Twelfth-century Saint Francis of Assisi is revered as a man who saw God revealed in nature.

Variant forms include: *Fran, Frank* and *Frankie*.

Françoise

This girl's name is a French variant of *Frances*. Predominately used in France, the name means 'woman from France or free woman'.

Frank

This name is a shortened form of *Francis, Frances* or *Franklin*. Although it is more commonly borne by boys, it is also used as a name for girls. *Frankie* is a very popular variant, especially for girls.

Variant forms include: *Franc, Franck, Franco, Franky, Frantz* and *Franz*.

Franklin

The boy's name Franklin is of German and English origin and means 'landholder'. It is also a variant form of *Frank*. US President Franklin Roosevelt (1882-1945) is a famous bearer of the name.

Variant forms include: *Frank, Franklinn, Franklyn* and *Franklynn*.

Franz

A German and Italian variant of the boy's name *Francis*. Franz means 'Frenchman or free man'. It is a popular Roman Catholic name in countries that are German speaking.

Fraser

Of Scottish and French origin, the boy's name Fraser means 'forest men'. Some sources also suggest it may mean 'curly hair'. The popular American sitcom *Frasier* broadcast from 1993-2004, featuring the psychiatrist Fraser Crane.

Variant forms include: *Fraser, Frazer* and *Frazier*.

Fred

This boy's name is a variant of the Old German name *Frederick*, and the Old English name *Alfred*. It means 'a ruler who is peaceful'. Some sources suggest it may also mean 'wise counsel'.

Freda

This girl's name is of German origin and means 'peace or peace loving'. It may also mean 'protection and safety'. The variant forms *Frida* and *Frieda* are popular in Spain.

Frederick

This boy's name is of Old German origin and means 'a ruler who is peace loving' or 'rich and powerful ruler'. *Frederica* is the female equivalent of Frederick.

Variant forms include: *Eric*, *Fred*, *Fredd*, *Frederico*, *Freddie*, *Friedrich* and *Fritz*.

Freya

This girl's name is of Scandinavian origin and means 'a lady who is noble'. In Norse mythology Freya is the goddess of love and fertility, and Friday was named in her honour.

Fraya is a variant form.

Top Ten Names Beginning with F

GIRLS	BOYS
FLORENCE	FINLEY
FAITH	FINLAY
FRANCESCA	FREDDIE
FERN	FINN
FREYA	FRANK

Gabriel

The boy's name Gabriel is of Hebrew origin and means 'hero of God' or 'God is my strength'. In the Bible the name is borne by the archangel that appears to Mary to announce the birth of Christ.

Variant forms include: *Gab, Gabbi, Gabbie, Gabby, Gabe, Gabi, Gabie, Gaby, Gavriel, Gavril* and *Gavrilo*.

Gabriella

This girl's name is of Hebrew origin and is a variant of the name *Gabriele*, which means 'heroine of God'. The name's popularity has been steadily increasing since the 1960s.

Variant forms include: *Gab, Gabbi, Gabbie, Gabriel* and *Gabriell*.

Gaia

This unusual girl's name is of Greek origin from the word 'Gaea' meaning 'goddess of the earth'. It is also borne by the daughter (b.1999) of Oscar-winning British actress Emma Thompson (b.1959).

Gareth

This boy's name is of Welsh origin and means 'gentle'. Although it was adopted by English speakers in the sixth century, the name still retains its Welsh flavour.

Variant forms include: *Garith, Garreth* and *Garyth*.

Garfield

This boy's name is of Old English origin and means 'spear field'. It is more commonly known today as the name of an overweight and orange-coloured, comic-strip cat, which was first published in 1978.

Garth

The boy's name Garth is of Welsh and Scandinavian origin. An occupational name that became a first name, it means 'garden keeper' or 'enclosure, protection from the garden'.

Variant forms include: *Gar* and *Gareth*.

Gary

This boy's name is of Welsh, Irish, German and Old English origin and means 'spear'. It could also be a pet form of the boys' names *Gareth* and *Gerald*.

Variant forms include: *Gar, Gari, Garey, Garrey, Garrie* and *Garry*.

Gavin

This boy's name is of Welsh and Scottish origin and means 'white, small and blessed hawk'. A variant form of the name appeared in Arthurian legend, Sir Gawain, a knight of the Round Table.

Variant forms include: *Gavan, Gaven, Gavyn, Gawain, Gawaine, Gawayn, Gawayne, Gwayn* and *Gwayne*.

Gemma

The girl's name Gemma is of Latin origin and means 'precious stone, gem or jewel'. For Roman Catholics, Saint Gemma Galgani (1878-1903) is the patron saint of students.

Variant forms include: *Gem* and *Jemma*.

Genevieve

This girl's name is of French, German and Welsh origin and means 'white wave' or 'lady of the people, tribal woman'. Saint Genevieve (422-512) is the patron saint of Paris.

Variant forms include: *Gena, Genivieve, Gennie, Genny, Gina, Jennie* and *Jenny*.

Geoffrey

This boy's name is a variant of the Old German name *Jeffrey*, and means 'peace' or 'peaceful ruler'. The name was probably introduced by the Normans to England in the eleventh century.

Variant forms include: *Geffrey, Geoff, Geoffery* and *Geoffroy*.

George

This boy's name is of Greek origin and means 'farmer' or 'earth worker'. The third-century Saint George, immortalised in the dragon-slaying tale, is the patron saint of England.

Variant forms include: *Geordi, Geordie, Georg, Georges, Georgi, Georgie, Georgio, Georgios, Georgy, Gyorgy* and *Gyuri*.

Georgette

The girl's name Georgette is of Ancient Greek and French origin and means 'farmer' or 'worker of the earth'. It is the French feminine form of *George*.

Variant forms include: *Georgia* and *Georgetta*.

Georgia

This girl's name is the feminine form of *George* and it is of Greek and Latin origin. It means 'farmer' or 'earth worker', and is often known by its pet form *Georgie*.

Variant forms include: *Georgina* and *Gina*.

Georgina

The girl's name Georgina is of Latin origin and is a variant of *Georgia*, the feminine form of *George*. A popular variant of the name is *Gina*.

Geraint

The boy's name Geraint is of Latin origin and means 'old' and, by implication, the wisdom that comes with age. Sir Geraint appears in some Arthurian legends.

Variant forms include: *Gerant* and *Jerant*.

Gerald

The boy's name Gerald is of Old German origin and means 'spear ruler' or 'spear rule'. The name was introduced to England by the Normans in the eleventh century.

Variant forms include: *Gary, Gerard* and *Jerry*.

Geraldine

The feminine form of *Gerald*, the uncommon girl's name Geraldine has its origins in Old French and Old Germanic languages and means 'spear rule' or 'spear ruler'.

Variant forms include: *Geri, Jeraldine* and *Jeri*.

Gerard

The boy's name Gerard is of Old English origin and means 'brave spear', or 'one who is brave with the spear'. It is also the name of various saints.

Variant forms include: *Garrett, Gerald, Gerrard, Gerry* and *Jared*.

Germain

This boy's name is of Latin and French origin and means 'brotherly'. The feminine form of the name is *Germaine*, which could, perhaps, be said to mean 'sisterly'.

Giles

The boy's name Giles is of Ancient Greek origin and means 'young goat', or 'goat skin' in reference to the tough skins that ancient shields were once made of.

Variant forms include: *Gyles* and *Jyles*.

Gillian

The girl's name Gillian is of Latin origin and means 'youth' or 'youthful'. The name could have developed as a feminine form of *Julian*, or an elaboration of *Jill*.

Variant forms include: *Gill, Gillie* and *Jillian*.

Gina

The girl's name Gina is a feminine form of *Gene*, or a variant of *Jean*. It is also a pet name for *Angelina, Georgina* and *Georgia*. In Japan the meaning of Gina is 'silvery'.

Variant forms include: *Genna, Jena* and *Jenna*.

Ginger

This girl's name is of English origin and is literally from the word 'ginger', implying the plant or someone with flame-coloured hair. It has also evolved to mean 'liveliness', and is famously associated with the American actress, and Fred Astaire's dance partner, Ginger Rogers (1911-95).

Glen

This boy's name is of Irish and Gaelic origin and refers to a 'glen': the name for a valley between hills. It may also mean 'one who is from the valley'.

Variant forms include: *Glenn, Glennard, Glennie, Glennon, Glenny, Glin, Glinn, Glyn* and *Glynn*.

Glenis

The girl's name Glenis is now fairly uncommon. It is of Welsh origin and it is related to the name *Glen*. It means 'one who is from the valley'.

Variant forms include: *Glennis, Glenys, Glinnis, Glinyce, Glinys, Glinyss, Glynis* and *Glynnis*.

Gloria

This girl's name is of Latin origin and means 'glory'. The name was adopted by English speakers in the early twentieth century after one of the characters in the *George Bernard* Shaw play *You Never Can Tell* (1889).

Top Ten Names After Precious Stones & Metals

GIRLS	BOYS
RUBY	FLINT
GEMMA	ROCK
SAPPHIRE	STEELE
JADE	STONE
CRYSTAL	JASPER

Glyn

This boy's name is a Celtic variant of the Irish and Gaelic name *Glen*. The meaning of Glen is 'from the valley'. The Welsh variant of the name is *Glynn*.

Goldie

This girl's name is a variant of the Old English name *Golda*, which means 'precious metal'. Oscar-winning, American comedy actress Goldie Hawn (b.1945) is a famous bearer of the name.

Gordon

This boy's name is of Old English and Celtic origin and means 'large fortress'. It may also mean 'hill near a meadow'. The name is derived from a Scottish family name of a great clan.

Gordan is a variant form.

Grace

This girl's name is of Latin origin and means 'favour' or 'charm' or 'blessing'. For Christians the meaning of the name is associated with the 'grace of God'.

Gracie is a variant form.

Grant

The boy's name Grant is of English and Gaelic origin and means 'large and tall'. The name was first adopted by English speakers in the nineteenth century and has been popularised in recent years by Grant Mitchell, a character in the long-running BBC soap opera *EastEnders,* first broadcast in 1985.

Grantley is a variant form.

Grayson

This uncommon boy's name is of Old English origin and means 'son of the grey-haired man' or 'son of the steward'. The controversial English artist Grayson Perry (b.1960) and American singer Grayson Chance (b.1997) are famous bearers.

Variant forms include: *Graysen* and *Greyson.*

Gregory

The boy's name Gregory is of Greek origin and means 'vigilant and watchful'. Legendary American movie star Gregory Peck (1916–2003) was a famous bearer of the name.

Variant forms include: *Greg, Greger, Gregg* and *Greggory.*

Gus

The boy's name Gus is a shortened form of the more formal Latin name *Augustus*, which means 'worthy of respect'. It is also a shortened form of the name *Angus*.

Variant forms include: *Guss* and *Gustave.*

Guy

This boy's name is of Old German origin and has several meanings, including 'wood', 'warrior' or 'guide and leader'. The name is associated with the wicked Guy of Gisbourne in the Robin Hood legends, and Guy Fawkes who tried to blow up the Houses of Parliament in 1605.

Gwen

This girl's name, a shortened form of *Gwendolyn*, is of Welsh origin and means 'fair, white, holy and blessed'. Although widely adopted by English speakers, the name has strong Welsh associations.

Variant forms include: *Gwenda, Gwenn, Gwyn* and *Gwynn.*

Gwendolyn

This uncommon girl's name is of Welsh origin and means 'magical ring'. It may also mean 'one with a fair bow'. It is more common in its popular variant form *Wendy*.

Variants include: *Gwen, Gwenda, Gwyn* and *Gwyneth*.

Gwyn

This unisex name is of Welsh origin and means 'fair, blessed and holy'. It is also a shortened form of the girl's name *Gwyneth*. In England it is more popular as a girl's name.

Variant forms include: *Gwin* and *Gwinn*.

Gwyneth

This girl's name is of Welsh origin and means 'happiness and luck'. In recent years it has been associated with the Oscar-winning, American actress Gwyneth Paltrow (b.1972).

Variant forms include: *Gwyn, Gwynith* and *Winnie*.

Top Ten Names Beginning with G

GIRLS	BOYS
GRACE	GABRIEL
GRACIE	GARETH
GEORGIA	GRANT
GABRIELLA	GEORGE
GEORGINA	GORDON

Halle

This girl's name is a variant of the Old German name *Harriet* and means 'ruler'. It has come to prominence in recent years due to Oscar-winning, American actress Halle Berry (b.1966).

Hallie is a variant form.

Hamilton

This boy's name is of Old English origin and means 'grassy hill', or 'from the proud or home-lover's estate'. Hamilton is an unusual and relatively rare boy's name.

Variant forms include: *Hamel, Hamelton, Hamil* and *Hamill.*

Hamish

This boy's name is of Scottish origin and a variant of the Hebrew *James*, which means 'he who supplants'. The name was adopted by English speakers in the nineteenth century, but retains its strong Scottish associations.

Hammond

The unusual boy's name Hammond is of Old English origin and means 'chief protector' or 'protector of the home'.

Hana

The girl's name Hana is of Spanish, Japanese, Hawaiian, Arabic and Slavic origin and means 'enjoyment'. In Japanese it means 'flower and blossom'. It is also a popular Spanish variant of *Hannah.*

Hank

This boy's name is of Old German origin and means 'ruler of the home'. Since the seventeenth century it has also been known as a shortened form of *Henry.*

Hannah

This popular girl's name is of Hebrew origin and means 'grace' or 'God is gracious'. In the Old Testament Hannah is the mother of the prophet Samuel.

Variant forms include: *Ann, Anna, Anne, Annie, Hana, Hanah, Hanalee, Hanalise, Hanna, Hanne, Hannele, Hannelore, Hannie, Hanny* and *Honna*.

Hardy

This boy's name is of Old German origin and means 'brave, hardy and bold'. Since the beginning of the twentieth century the name has evolved from the transferred use of a surname.

Hardey is a variant form.

Harley

The popular boy's name Harley is of Old English origin and means 'hare meadow'. It may also mean 'rocky or long meadow'. The name is familiar to many people because of the iconic motorcycle, the Harley-Davidson.

Variant forms include: *Harlea, Harlee, Harleigh* and *Harly*.

Harold

The Anglo-Saxon name Harold is of Scandinavian origin and means 'army ruler' or 'warrior among men'. In its variant form *Herald*, it means 'one who proclaims'.

Variant forms include: *Hal, Harald, Haralds, Harolda, Haroldo, Harrell* and *Harry*.

Harriet

The girl's name Harriet is the feminine form of *Harry*. It is of Old German origin and means 'powerful ruler of the home'. It is also an informal version of *Henrietta*.

Variant forms include: *Halle, Hallie, Harrie, Harriett, Harriot, Harriott, Harriotte, Hatsee, Hattie* and *Hatty*.

Harrison

This boy's name is of Old English origin and means 'son of *Harry*'. In recent years its popularity has been boosted by the success of American actor Harrison Ford (b.1942).

Variant forms include: *Harris, Harriss* and *Harrisson*.

Harry

The enduringly popular boy's name Harry is of Old English origin and means 'powerful ruler of the home'. In recent years the name's popularity has been boosted by Prince Harry (b.1984), as well as by Harry Potter, the boy hero of the hugely successful *Harry Potter* (1997-2007) series of novels by J. K. Rowling.

Variant forms include: *Hal* and *Harrie*.

Harvey

The popular boy's name Harvey is of Old English, Celtic and Old French origin and means 'one who is eager for battle' or 'one who is strong and worthy in battle'.

Variant forms include: *Harv, Harve, Harvee, Harvie, Harvy* and *Hervey*.

Top Ten Christmas-Related Names

GIRLS	BOYS
ANGEL	NICHOLAS
MARY	JOSEPH
CAROL	NOEL
JOY	JESUS
HOLLY	RUDOLF

Hayden

This boy's name is of Old English origin and means 'heathen' or 'hedged valley'. It is associated with the Canadian actor Hayden Christensen (b.1981), who played Darth Vader in the second and third *Star Wars* prequels (2002, 2005).

Variant forms include: *Haden, Haydan, Haydn* and *Haydon.*

Hayley

This girl's name is of Old English origin and means 'hay meadow'. It was made famous by the popularity of Oscar-winning, British actress Hayley Mills (b.1946).

Variant forms include: *Hailey, Haley, Halie, Hally, Haylea, Haylee* and *Hayleigh.*

Hazel

This popular girl's name is of Old English origin and means 'the hazel tree'. It is among several flower and plant names coined and adopted in the late-nineteenth century by English speakers.

Variant forms include: *Hazal, Hazell, Hazelle* and *Hazle.*

Heath

The unisex name Heath is more commonly used for boys. It is of Middle English origin and means 'heath', a place of untended land where plants can freely grow.

Variant forms include: *Heathe, Heeth, Heith* and *Heth.*

Heather

The ever popular girl's name Heather, or *Hether*, is of Middle English origin and means 'heather', the evergreen flowering plant that can survive in barren landscapes.

Hebe

This unusual girl's name is of Ancient Greek origin and means 'youth and young'. In Greek mythology Hebe is the goddess of youth and cupbearer to the gods, serving them nectar and ambrosia.

Hector

This boy's name is of Greek origin and means 'one who is steadfast' or 'one who can hold strong'. Hector was the prince of Troy in Homer's *Illiad,* one of the oldest written works in Europe, dated to around the eighth century BC.

Hedley

The unisex name Hedley is of Old English origin and is a variant of *Hadley.* It means 'heather meadow' or 'clearing of heather'. It is an unusual name.

Variant forms include: *Headleigh, Headley, Headly* and *Hedly.*

Heidi

This popular girl's name is a shortened form of *Adelaide* and means 'noble and kind'. It is familiar to many as the name of the girl in Johanna Spyri's beloved children's novel *Heidi* (1880).

Variant forms include: *Heidey, Heidy* and *Hydee.*

Helen

This girl's name is of Greek origin and means 'bright one, shining light'. In mythology, Helen of Troy's famed beauty resulted in the Trojan War - she became the 'face that launched a thousand ships'.

Variant forms include: *Eleanor, Ella, Ellen, Ellie, Elnora, Helaine, Helena, Helenann, Helene, Helenna, Ilona, Lana, Leanora, Lena, Lenore, Leonora, Leonore* and *Leora.*

Helena

This all-time favourite girl's name is a variant of the Ancient Greek names *Helen* and *Eleanor.* Helen means 'shining light'. *Alena* is a German variant of the name.

Henrietta

This girl's name is of Old German origin and means 'rich, powerful ruler of the home'. It is the feminine form of *Henry*, and a more formal variant form of *Harriet*.

Variant forms include: *Etta, Ettie, Etty, Hattie, Hatty, Henrieta, Henriette, Hette* and *Hettie*.

Henry

This widely used and popular royal name for English and French king is of German origin. It means 'rich, powerful ruler of the home'. *Henri* is the French form of the name.

Variant forms include: *Hal, Hank, Harry, Heinz, Henrik, Henrique* and *Hinrich*.

Herbert

This boy's name is of Old German origin and means 'illustrious, bright or famed warrior'. The name is a variant of Saint Heribert (970-1021), who was Archbishop of Cologne.

Variant forms include: *Bert, Bertie, Herb* and *Herbie*.

Hermione

The girl's name Hermoine is of Greek origin and means 'messenger'. It was made famous in recent years as the name of a leading character in the hugely successful *Harry Potter* novels (1997-2007) by J. K. Rowling.

Variant forms include: *Herma, Hermia, Hermina, Hermine* and *Herminia*.

Hilary

This unisex name, although today it is far more commonly used for girls than for boys, is of Latin origin and means 'one who is cheerful and happy'.

Variant forms include: *Hillary, Hillery* and *Hilliary*.

Top Ten Successful Names

Names rated high on the
'Success In Life Scale' by UK psychologists.

GIRLS	BOYS
ELIZABETH	JAMES
CAROLINE	MICHAEL
HELEN	ANDREW
OLIVIA	WILLIAM
AMANDA	RICHARD

Hilda

The girl's name Hilda is of Old German origin and a short form of *Hildegard*. It means 'warrior woman'. Saint Hilda was a much respected, seventh-century abbess in England.

Variant forms include: *Hilde, Hildie* and *Hylda*.

Holly

A popular name for girls, Holly (also popular as the variant *Hollie*) is of Old English origin and means 'holly tree' - the evergreen shrub or tree. It may also have associations with the word 'holy'. The name is often given to girls born at or near Christmas.

Variant forms include: *Hollee, Holleigh, Holley, Holli, Hollie* and *Hollye*.

Homer

This unusual boy's name is of Greek origin and means 'helmet maker' or 'hostage'. Familiar to many as the name of Homer Simpson, the famous character in the American animated TV sitcom *The Simpsons* (1989 - present).

Honor

This girl's name is of Latin origin. It is derived, literally, from the word honour and means 'a woman of honour'. It is associated with the British actress Honor Blackman (b.1925).

Variant forms include: *Nora* and *Norah*.

Hope

This girl's name is of Old English origin and means 'expectation and belief'. Along with *Faith* and *Charity*, it is one of three named Christian virtues in the Bible at I Corinthians 13:13.

Howard

This boy's name, which was also a surname among Old English nobility, is of Old English origin and means 'warden who is noble'. *Howie* is a common shortened form of the name.

Hudson

This boy's name is of Old English origin and means 'son of Hudd or Hugh'. It was popularised in the USA by English explorer Henry Hudson (1570-1611), who lent his name to Hudson Bay.

Hugh

The boy's name Hugh is of Old German origin and means 'heart, mind and spirit'. It has been popularised in recent years by British actor Hugh Grant (b.1960).

Variant forms include: *Hughes, Hughie* and *Hugo*.

Hugo

The boy's name Hugo is of Old German and Latin origin and a common variant of *Hugh*, which means 'heart, mind and spirit'. It is also the English variant form of *Hubert*.

Hunter

Although Hunter is a unisex name, it is a more popular choice for boys than girls. It is of Old English origin and means 'pursuer or hunter'. *Hunt* is a shortened form of the name.

Hyacinth

This girl's name is of Greek origin and refers to a 'hyacinth', a flower that blooms in a variety of colours. The name was boosted by Hyacinth Bucket, an eccentric lady in the BBC sitcom *Keeping Up Appearances* (1990-95).

Variant forms include: *Cintha, Cinthia, Cinthie, Cinthy, Hyacinthe, Hyacinthia* and *Hyacinthie.*

Hywel

The boy's name Hywel is of Old Welsh origin and means 'one who is eminent and alert'. Primarily a Welsh name, *Howell* and *Hywell* are English variants.

Top Ten Names Beginning with H

GIRLS	BOYS
HOLLY	HARRY
HANNAH	HARVEY
HEIDI	HARRISON
HARRIET	HENRY
HOLLIE	HARLEY

Ian

The boy's name Ian is a variant of the Scottish name *John*, which means 'God is gracious'. It is now widely used among English speakers and no longer so strongly associated with its Scottish origins.

Variant spellings include: *Iain* and *Ion*.

Ibrahim

This rather popular boy's name is of Arabic origin and a variant of the Dutch, English, German and Hebrew name *Abraham*, which means 'father of many'.

Ibraheem is a variant form.

Imelda

This unusual girl's name is of German and Italian origin and means 'universal battle'. It has been made famous by Imelda Marcos (b.1929), the former Philippine first lady.

Imogen

The uncommon girl's name Imogen is of Irish and Gaelic origin and means 'innocent maiden'. The name was adopted by English speakers in the late-nineteenth century.

India

The girl's name India is of English origin and refers to the name of the country. The name was adopted by English speakers in the late-nineteenth century, when India was a colony of the British Empire.

Indiana

The girl's name Indiana is of Latin origin and means 'from India'. Although it is a girl's name, in the *Indiana Jones* movies (1981-2008), the fictional American adventurer Indiana Jones is a man.

Indigo

This unisex name, which is more commonly used for girls, is of English origin and refers to the colour indigo (deep dark blue), which is itself of Greek origin.

Indra

This unisex name has its origins in the Sanskrit language and is used largely in India. It means 'possessing, or owning, large drops of rain'. The name is borne by the Hindu Lord of Rain.

Variant forms: *Indira* and *Indrani*.

Ingmar

This rare unisex name is of Russian and Scandinavian origin and means 'great or famous'. The name was borne by the celebrated Swedish film director Ingmar Bergman (1918-2007).

Ingrid

The girl's name Ingrid is of Old Norse origin and means 'Inq's ride' or 'the beauty of Inq'. Inq was the god of the earth's fertility. It is associated with the Swedish screen legend Ingrid Bergman (1915-1982).

Top Ten Names Associated with Colour

GIRLS	BOYS
SKY	INDIGO
ROSE	BRUNO
SIENNA	JET
VIOLET	RUSTY
FERN	JASPER

Ira

This unusual and uncommon unisex name is of Hebrew origin and means 'watchful' or 'one who is fully grown'. It is more popular in its variant form *Irene.*

Irene

The girl's name Irene is of Greek origin and means 'peaceful'. In Greek mythology Irene is the personification and goddess of peace. The name's popularity peaked in the early twentieth century.

Variant forms include: *Ira, Ireen, Iren, Irena, Irenea, Irenee* and *Rina.*

Iris

This girl's name is of Greek origin and means 'rainbow'. It also refers to the flower of the same name and the iris of the eye, which is so named for its multiple colours.

Irma

The unusual girl's name Irma is of German origin and means 'immense or universal'. Both Irma and its variant *Erma* are uncommon names in English-speaking countries.

Isaac

The boy's name Isaac is of Hebrew origin and means 'laughter'. In the Old Testament, Isaac is the only son of *Abraham* and *Sarah.*

Variant forms include:, *Isac, Issac, Isaak, Zack* and *Zak.*

Isabel

The hugely popular girl's name Isabel is of Hebrew origin and means 'God's promise'. It has numerous variant forms, with the most popular being *Isabella, Isabelle* and *Isobel.* The name is also a Spanish variant of *Elizabeth.* Various forms of the name have been borne by royalty and royal consorts.

Variant forms include: *Bell, Bella, Belle, Isabela, Isabele, Isabell, Isabella, Isabelle, Isbel, Isobel, Isobell, Isobella, Isobelle, Issie, Issy, Izabel, Izabella, Izabelle, Izzie* and *Izzy.*

Isadora

This girl's name is of Greek and Latin origin and means 'gift of Isis'. Isis was an ancient and powerful Egyptian goddess. The expressive American dancer Isadora Duncan (1877-1927) was a famous bearer of this name.

Isla

The unusual girl's name Isla is of Scottish origin and is the name of a Scottish river. It is mainly used in Scotland and is sometimes considered a shortened form of *Isabella*.

Ivan

The boy's name Ivan is of Russian and Slavic origin and a variant of the Hebrew name *John*, which means 'God is gracious'. It was borne by rulers of Russia.

Variant forms include: *Ivanhoe* and *Iwan*.

Ivor

This boy's name is of Scandinavian and Old Norse origin and means 'archer, soldier, bow man or bow army'. In Welsh, Ifor is associated with the word meaning 'lord'.

Variant forms include: *Egor, Igor, Ivar* and *Iver*.

Ivy

The girl's name Ivy is of English origin and is the name of the evergreen, climbing plant. *Ivo* is the masculine form of the name. It was adopted by English speakers during the late-nineteenth century during the vogue for plant and flower names as first names.

Variant forms include: *Iva, Ivee, Ivey* and *Ivie*.

Top Ten Names Beginning with I

GIRLS	BOYS
ISABELLE	ISSAC
ISABELLA	IAN
IMOGEN	IBRAHIM
ISOBEL	IVAN
ISABEL	INDIANA

Jack

This widely used boy's name is of Old English origin and means 'God's grace' or 'God is gracious'. For over a decade it has held the number one spot for boys' names in the UK.

Variant forms include: *Jackie, Jackman, Jacko, Jacky, Jacques, Jak* and *Jaq*.

Jackie

This unisex name is of English and Hebrew origin and a variant of the hugely popular name *Jack*. It means 'son of Jack' and 'God's mercy'. It is also a pet form of the girl's name *Jacqueline*.

Variant forms include: *Jackee, Jackey, Jacki, Jacky, Jacque, Jacqui* and *Jacquie*.

Jackson

The boy's name Jackson is of Old English origin and means 'son of Jack'. American President Andrew Jackson (1767-1845) promoted the popularity of the name.

Variant forms include: *Jack, Jackie, Jacksen, Jacky, Jakson, Jax, Jaxen, Jaxon* and *Jaxson*.

Jacob

The boy's name Jacob is of Hebrew origin and means 'to follow or track' or 'to supplant'. In the Bible Jacob is the father of twelve sons who went on to found the twelve tribes of Israel.

Variant forms include: *Jack, Jackie, Jacko, Jacky, Jacques, Jake, Jakeb, Jakie, Jakob, Jakov, Jim, Jimmie* and *Yakov*.

Jacqueline

This girl's name is of French origin, and the feminine version of *James*, which means 'he who supplants'. The name was first used by English speakers in the thirteenth century.

Variant forms include: *Jackie, Jaclyn* and *Jacquelyn*.

Jade

This popular unisex jewel name is of English origin and means 'precious stone'. Jade is a semi-precious green stone. The name's popularity was boosted when English rock singer Mick Jagger (b.1943) named his daughter Jade Jagger (b.1971).

Variant forms include: *Jaden, Jadeyn, Jadien, Jadine, Jadyn, Jaide, Jaiden, Jayde* and *Jayden*.

Jake

The popular boy's name Jake is of English origin. It is a shortened form of *Jacob* and a variant of *Jack*. It developed in the Middle Ages, and went on to become a name in its own right.

James

The boy's name James is of English origin and a variant of the Hebrew name *Jacob*, which means 'he who supplants'. It is a classic that continues to be widely used.

Variant forms include: *Jamie, Jim, Jimmie* and *Jimmy*.

Jamie

The popular name Jamie is a diminutive of *James* and has become an independent name. It is a unisex name, but a more popular choice today for girls than boys.

Variant forms include: *Jaime, Jaimie, Jamee, Jamey* and *Jayme*.

Jan

This unisex name is of Hebrew origin and means 'with the grace of God'. It is also a short form for *Janet* and *Janice*, a variant of *Jane*, and a feminine form of *John*.

Variant forms include: *Jana, Janah, Janine, Jann, Janna, Jannah* and *Janne*.

Jane

This enduringly popular girl's name is of Hebrew origin and was originally a feminine form of *John*. It means 'God's grace or God is mercy'. It is the name of the independent-minded central character in Charlotte Brontë's classic romantic novel *Jane Eyre* (1847).

Variant forms include: *Janeen, Janel, Janela, Janelba, Janella, Janelle, Janean, Janeane, Janee, Janene, Janerita, Janessa, Janet, Janette, Janey, Janice, Janie, Jean* and *Joan*.

Janet

This girl's name is of Hebrew origin and a widely used medieval diminutive of the name *Jane*. After the Middle Ages its popularity fell, but it was revived again in nineteenth-century Scotland.

Variant forms include: *Janett, Janetta, Janette, Jennet* and *Jennette*.

Janice

This girl's name is of Hebrew and English origin and a variant of *Jane*. It may have made its first appearance as the name of the heroine in Paul Leicester Ford's novel *Janice Meredith* (1899).

Variant forms include: *Janis, Janise, Janiss, Jannice, Jannis, Janyce, Jenice, Jeniece, Jenise* and *Jennice*.

Janine

The girl's name Janine is of Hebrew and English origin and is a variant of *Jean, Jeanine* and *Jane*. It means 'God is gracious' or 'God is merciful'.

Variant forms include: *Janene, Janina, Jannina* and *Jannine*.

Jared

The boy's name Jared is of Hebrew origin and means 'to descend'. The name was adopted by Puritans in the seventeenth century and saw a revival in the 1960s.

Variant forms include: *Jarad, Jarid, Jarod, Jarrad, Jarrard, Jarred, Jarrid, Jarrod, Jerred* and *Jerrod*.

Popular Boys Names
in China

TAO	MA
AN	DA
CHENG	TA
HUI	KAI
LIANG	LANG

Jarvis

The boy's name Jarvis is a variant of the Old German name *Gervase*, which means 'one with honour'. It may also mean 'a spear'. The controversial British musician Jarvis Cocker (b.1963) is a well-known bearer of this name.

Jasmine

This girl's name is of Old French and Old Persian origin and it refers to jasmine, the fragrant flower used to make perfume. It was adopted by English speakers in the late-nineteenth century during the vogue for plant and flower names, and was made famous by the Princess Jasmine character in the popular Walt Disney animation *Aladdin* (1992).

Variant forms include: *Jas, Jasmin, Jasmina, Jasminda, Jasmyn, Jasmyne, Jassamayn, Jazzmin, Jazzmine, Jazzmon, Jazzmyn, Jazzmynn* and *Jess*.

Jason

The boy's name Jason is of Greek and Hebrew origin and means 'healer' or 'God is my salvation'. The name was borne by the legendary Greek hero Jason, who led a group of warriors called the Argonauts.

Variant forms include: *Jasen, Jasin, Jasun, Jay, Jaysen* and *Jayson*.

Jasper

The boy's name Jasper is of Greek and Persian origin and means 'keeper of the treasure'. Jasper is also a semi-precious red (and brown) coloured gemstone that is harder than glass.

Variant forms include: *Caspar, Gaspar, Jaspar* and *Jesper*.

Jay

This unisex name is of Latin origin and means 'blue-crested bird'. Some sources suggest it may mean 'happy'. It is also a nickname for most names beginning with the letter J.

Variant forms include: *Jae* and *Jaye*.

Jayden

This unisex name is a variant of the ancient Hebrew name *Jadon*, which means 'God is listening'. Considered trendy by many, its popularity has been steadily increasing since the late 1990s.

Variant forms include: *Jade, Jaden* and *Jaydon*.

Jean

Although this name is unisex, it is more common as a girl's name. It is of Hebrew origin and means 'God's Grace'. Jean is also a variant of the popular girl's name *Jane*.

Variant forms include: *Gene, Jeana, Jeanne, Jeanine, Jeanne, Jeanette, Jeannette, Jeannie, Jeannine* and *Jennine*.

Jefferson

This boy's name is of Old English origin and means 'son of Jeffery'. Jefferson is a classic name and although it was used more widely in the past, it is still fairly popular today in the United States.

Variant forms include: *Jeff, Jeffers, Jeffersson, Jeffey* and *Jeffie*.

Jeffrey

This boy's name is of Old German origin and means 'peace'. It has been in use since the Middle Ages and is probably a variant of the boy's name *Geoffrey*.

Variant forms include: *Jeff, Jefferey, Jefferies, Jefferson, Jeffery, Jeffree, Jeffries, Jeffy* and *Jefry*.

Jemima

The girl's name Jemima is of Hebrew origin and means 'dove' or 'bright as day'. In the Old Testament Jemima is the eldest daughter of Job and considered the most beautiful woman in the world.

Jennifer

The widely used girl's name Jennifer is of Welsh origin and means 'fair one'. Often shortened to *Jenny*, it is a variant of the Old French name *Guinevere* – King Arthur's legendary queen.

Variant forms include: *Jen, Jena, Jenefer, Jeni, Jenifer, Jeniffer, Jenn, Jenna, Jenni, Jennica, Jennie, Jenniver, Jenny* and *Jinny*.

Jenny

The name Jenny first appeared as a variant of the names *Jean* or *Jane* in the Middle Ages, but since the late-nineteenth century it has been known as a shortened form of *Jennifer*.

Jeremy

This boy's name is a variant of the Hebrew name Jeremiah, which means 'the Lord exaults' or 'lift up the Lord'. The name was borne by an important prophet in the Bible, who wrote the book of Jeremiah in the Old Testament.

Variant forms include: *Jem, Jemmie, Jemmy* and *Jerry*.

Jerome

This boy's name is of Greek origin and means 'sacred name' or 'one who bears a sacred name'. Used since the twelfth century by English speakers, Jerome remains a classic favourite.

Variant forms include: *Gerry* and *Jerry*.

Jerry

This unisex name is of English origin and a shortened form of names that begin with 'Jer'. It is now used as an independent name. It is also a pet form of *Gerald* and *Gerard*.

Variant forms include: *Gerry, Jerre, Jerrey* and *Jerrie*.

Jesse

This unisex name is of Hebrew origin and means 'the Lord exists' or 'He sees'. Jesse is also a variant form of the very popular girl's name *Jessica*.

Variant forms include: *Jess, Jessey, Jessie, Jessy* and *Yishai*.

Jessica

This hugely popular girl's name is of Hebrew origin and means 'God sees or beholds' or 'foresight'. The name Jessica seems to have been coined by William Shakespeare as the name for Shylock's daughter in his play *The Merchant of Venice* (written between 1596 and 1598).

Variant forms include: *Jess, Jesse, Jesseca, Jessey, Jessie, Jessika* and *Jessy*.

Top Ten Names in the USA in 2009

GIRLS	BOYS
ISABELLA	JACOB
EMMA	ETHAN
OLIVIA	MICHAEL
SOPHIA	ALEXANDER
AVA	WILLIAM

Jessie

This unisex name, though it is slightly more popular for girls, is a variant form of the girl's names *Jessica* and *Jean*, and the unisex name *Jesse*. It was taken up by English speakers in the nineteenth century.

Jet

The boy's name Jet is of English and Greek origin and means 'to throw'. It also refers to the colour 'jet black' and to 'jet', the shiny black substance which was used in the Victorian era for mourning jewellery.

Variant forms include: *Jett* and *Jette*.

Jill

The girl's name Jill comes from the Latin name *Juliana,* which means 'young'. It is also a shortened form of the girl's name *Gillian*. The name is familiar to many from the enduringly popular eighteenth-century nursery rhyme 'Jack and Jill'.

Jim

This boy's name is a medieval variant of the Hebrew boy's name *James*. It was made famous by the character Jim Hawkins in Robert Louis Stevenson's novel *Treasure Island* (1883).

Variant forms include: *Jimmey, Jimmie, Jimmy* and *Jimson*.

Jimmy

The boy's name Jimmy is a variant of the names *Jamie* and *James*, which means 'God will protect', as well as *Jim*. It went on to become an independent name.

Jo

This unisex name is a variant of the Hebrew boy's name *Joseph*, which means 'God increases' and the English girl's name *Joanne*. *Joe* tends to be a boy-only variant.

Variant forms include: *Joel* and *Joey*.

Joan

This girl's name is of Hebrew origin and means 'God's grace'. It is famously associated with Saint Joan of Arc, a fifteenth-century teenage heroine who led the French army to victory against the English.

Variant forms include: *Joane, Joanie* and *Joni.*

Joanna

The girl's name Joanna is an English variant of the names *Jean* and *Jane*. Usually spelled *Johanna* in the Middle Ages, the form Joanna became more popular in the nineteenth century.

Variant forms include: *Jo, Joana, Joanie, Joann, Jo-Ann, Joanne, Jo-Anne, Joeann, Joeanna* and *Joeanne.*

Joanne

The girl's name Joanne is a variant of the name *Joanna*. J.K. Rowling (b.1965), the bestselling author of the *Harry Potter* novels is a famous bearer of the name.

Jody

This unisex name is of Hebrew and English origin. It is a nickname – that went on to become an independent name – for the following names: *Joseph, Jude, Joan, Judith, Joanna, Josephine* and *Jo*.

Variant forms include: *Jodee, Jodey, Jodi* and *Jodie.*

Joel

The boy's name Joel is of Hebrew origin and means 'God is the Lord'. In the Bible, in the Old Testament, Joel is a prophet and writer of the book of Joel in the eighth century BC.

John

The ever-popular boy's name John is of Hebrew origin and means 'God is gracious'. The term 'John Bull' was created in 1712 by Scottish writer John Arbuthnot (1667-1735) to describe the archetypal Englishman. *Jane* is the feminine form of John.

Variant forms include: *Jack, Jan, Jean, Jon* and *Jock.*

Jolene

The girl's name Jolene could be a modern variant of the boy's name *Joseph*, or it could be a combination of the names *Jo* and *Marlene*. In 1973, Dolly Parton recorded a hit song of the same name, making it famous.

Variant forms include: *Joeleen, Joeline, Joleen, Jolena, Jolina, Joline, Jolleen, Jollene* and *Jolyn*.

Jonah

This boy's name is of Hebrew origin and means 'dove' and 'peace'. In the popular Bible story, Jonas the prophet is thrown over the side of a ship and swallowed by a whale. In seafaring superstition, Jonah is one of the more feared names.

Jonas is a variant form.

Jonas

This boy's name is a variant of the Hebrew name *Jonah*, and means 'dove'. It also means 'peace' as the dove is a universally recognised symbol of peace.

Top Ten
Unisex Names

ALEX	JORDAN
CASEY	RILEY
DEVON	RORY
JADEN	SAM
JESS	TAYLOR

Jonathan

This popular boy's name is of Hebrew origin and means 'God's gift' or 'God has given'. In the Bible the name was borne by a close friend of King David and is therefore associated with devotion and friendship.

Variant forms include: *Johnathan, Johnathon, Jon* and *Jonathon.*

Jordan

This unisex name is of Hebrew origin with the meaning 'flowing down'. It is also the name of a sacred river in Palestine, where Jesus was baptised by John the Baptist.

Variant forms include: *Jared, Jarred, Jorden, Jordi, Jordon, Jordy* and *Jordyn.*

Joseph

The name Joseph is of Hebrew origin and means 'God increases'. In the Bible Joseph is the son of *Jacob* who, despite being sold into slavery by his brothers, rises to become a great power in Egypt. It is also the name of the husband of Mary, mother of Jesus.

Variant forms include: *Jo, Jody, Jose* and *Joss.*

Josephine

The girl's name Josephine is the feminine form of *Joseph*. It is of Hebrew origin and means 'God will add or increase'. African-American singer Josephine Baker (1906–75) is a famous bearer of the name.

Variant forms include: *Jo* and *Josie.*

Josh

The boy's name Josh is a shortened form of the Hebrew boy's name *Joshua*, which means 'God will save me' or 'God is my salvation'. The variant form *Joss* is steadily growing in popularity.

Joss

The unisex name Joss is a shortened form of the girl's name *Jocelyn*, which used to be a unisex name. English singer Joss Stone (b.1987) is a famous bearer of the name.

Variant forms include: *Josh, Joslin* and *Josslin.*

Joy

This girl's name is of Latin origin and means 'joy'. Although it used to represent the joy of Christianity, today it may simply suggests the parents' desire for their child to live a happy life.

Joyce is a variant form.

Jude

This boy's name is of Hebrew origin and a variant of the uncommon name *Judah*. It means 'praised' or 'one who is praised'. English actor Jude Law (b.1972) is a famous bearer of the name.

Judd is a variant form.

Judith

This girl's name is of Hebrew origin and means 'from Judea'. The name was used by English speakers prior to the Norman Conquest (1066) and has remained popular over the centuries.

Variant forms include: *Jodie, Jody, Judi, Judie* and *Judy.*

Judy

The girl's name Judy is a shortened form of the Hebrew girl's name *Judith*. American actress and singer Judy Garland (1922-69) was an international star.

Jules

This unisex name is a modern French and English variant of the Ancient Greek name *Julias*, which means 'love's child'. It is also a pet form of the girl's name *Julia*, and the boy's name *Julian*.

Julia

This very popular girl's name is of Latin origin and means 'young, love's child' or 'child of Jupiter'. Oscar-winning, American actress Julia Roberts (b.1967) is a famous bearer of the name.

Variant forms include: *Juliana, Juliane, Juliann, Julianne, Julie, Julienne* and *Juliet*.

Julian

The name Julian is of Greek origin and means 'love's child'. Previously a unisex name, it was adopted regularly by English speakers as a boy's name in the eighteenth century.

Variant forms include: *Jules* and *Julius*.

Juliana

This girl's name is of Latin origin and means 'love's child'. It may also mean 'youthful' or 'Jupiter's child'. It has been adopted by English speakers since the twelfth century.

Variant forms include: *Juliane, Juliann, Julianna, Julianne* and *Julieann*.

Julius

The boy's name Julius is of Greek origin and means 'love's or Jupiter's child'. The name is most often associated with the Roman general and statesman Gaius Julius Caesar (100-44 BC).

Julie

This girl's name is of French origin and a shortened form of *Julia*, which means 'love's or Jupiter's child'. It was regularly adopted by English speakers from the 1920s.

Variant forms include: *Juley, Julienne, Juliet* and *Jully*.

Juliet

This girl's name is a variant of *Julia* and means 'love's child'. It is forever associated with the star-crossed lover, Juliet, in William Shakespeare's play *Romeo and Juliet* (written between 1591 and 1595).

Variant forms include: *Julette, Julieta, Juliett, Julietta* and *Juliette*.

June

This girl's name is of English origin and refers to the month of 'June'. It was first used as a name by English speakers in the early twentieth century. *Juno* is a variant form growing in popularity.

Juno

This girl's name is of Latin and Celtic origin and means 'hunger'. In Roman mythology Juno was the queen of the gods, who was also the sister and wife of Jupiter.

June is a variant form.

Justin

This boy's name is of Latin origin and means 'one who is just, fair and righteous'. The name was borne by various early saints. *Justine* is the feminine form of the name.

Justen is a variant form.

Justine

The girl's name Justine is of Latin origin and derived from the word, 'justus', which means 'one who is righteous, fair and just'. It is the feminine form of *Justin*.

Variant forms include: *Justeen, Justeene, Justene, Justie, Justina* and *Justinn*.

Top Ten Names Beginning with J

GIRLS	BOYS
JESSICA	JACK
JASMINE	JOSHUA
JULIA	JAMES
JADE	JOSEPH
JORDAN	JACOB

Kai

The unisex name Kai is of Welsh, Scandinavian and Greek origin and means 'earth' and 'keeper of the keys'. In Hawaiian 'kai' means the sea.

Variant forms include: *Kay* and *Kye.*

Kane

The boy's name Kane is of Irish and Gaelic origin and means 'little battle'. In Hawaiian, Kane means 'man' or 'the eastern sky'. In Welsh the meaning is 'beautiful'.

Variant forms include: *Cain, Caine, Cane, Kain, Kaine, Kayne* and *Keane.*

Karen

This girl's name is of Greek origin and a shortened form of *Katherine*, which means 'pure'. This widely used name peaked in the mid-1950s and has since had a fall in popularity.

Variant forms include: *Caren, Carin, Caron, Caronn, Carren, Carrin, Carron, Karan, Karon, Karren, Keren,* and *Kerran.*

Kasey

This unisex name is of Celtic, Greek and American origin and means 'alert, vigilant, wakeful and energetic'. It is an alternative form of the Irish and Gaelic unisex name *Casey.*

Kate

The popular girl's name Kate is a shortened form of the name *Katherine*, now used as a name in its own right. *Katie* is another popular English shortened form of *Katherine*.

Variant forms include: *Cait, Caitie, Cate, Catee, Catey, Catie, Kaitlin, Katee* and *Katey.*

Katherine

The girl's name Katherine is of Ancient Greek origin and means 'pure'. There are also links to the word 'torture'. Records suggest that the name, and its many variants, may date back to at least the third century. Through the centuries, Katherine has consistently remained an all-time favourite girl's name.

Variant forms include: *Cait, Caitlin, Cate, Catherine, Kaitie, Kaitlin, Katharine, Kathleen, Kathlene, Kathy, Karen, Katriana, Katrina, Katrine, Katy* and *Kay*.

Kathleen

This girl's name is of Irish origin and a variant of the Ancient Greek name *Katherine*, which means 'pure'. Kathleen is a classic favourite name.

Variant forms include: *Cathleen, Caitlin* and *Kaitlin*.

Katrina

The girl's name Katrin is a variant shortened form of the Ancient Greek name *Katherine*, which means 'pure'. It is predominantly used by English, Finnish and German speakers.

Variant forms include: *Catrina* and *Catriona*.

Kay

This unisex name is a variant form of the Ancient Greek name *Katherine*, which means 'pure'. It has now become an independent name in its own right.

Variant forms include: *Kai, Kaye, Kayla, Kaylee* and *Kaylin*.

Kayden

Although a unisex name, Kayden is currently much more popular as a boy's name. It is of Celtic origin and means 'son'. The Arabic variant *Kaden* means 'companion'.

Kayley

The girl's name Kayley is of Gaelic origin and means 'slender'. In recent years it has become more popular due to the influence of similar sounding names, like *Kelly, Kylie* and *Kay*.

Variant forms include: *Caleigh, Cayleigh, Cayley, Kaelee, Kaeleigh, Kaeley, Kaeli, Kaelie, Kailee, Kaileigh, Kailey, Kaley, Kalie, Kaylee* and *Kaylley*.

Kayla

This girl's name is of Ancient Greek, Celtic and Hebrew origin and a variant form of the names *Katherine, Kayley* and *Kay*. It is also a pet form of *Michaela*.

Keane

The boy's name Keane is of Irish, Gaelic and Old English origin, and its meaning is 'sharp, keen wit'. It is also a variant form of the Celtic *Cian*, meaning 'ancient one'.

Variant forms include: *Kean, Keen, Keene* and *Keyne*.

Keeley

This unisex name, although it is more commonly used for girls, is of Celtic origin and predominantly used by English and Irish speakers. It means 'graceful, slender and pretty'.

Variant forms include: *Keely* and *Kelly*.

Keira

The girl's name Keira is a variant of the Celtic name *Ciara*, meaning 'dark-haired one', and the Greek *Kyra*, meaning 'lady'. British actress Keira Knightly (b.1985) – star of the Disney *Pirates of the Caribbean* movies (2003, 2006, 2007) – is a famous bearer of the name.

Keith

The boy's name Keith is of Scottish and Gaelic origin and means 'woodland or forest'. Until the nineteenth century the name was rare outside Scotland, but it has now been adopted by people with no Scottish connections.

Kelly

This unisex name is of Irish and Gaelic origin and it is derived from a word that means 'church or monastery'. Today it is a more popular name for girls than boys.

Variant forms include: *Kelley, Kelli* and *Kellie*.

Kelsey

This unisex name is more popular for girls than boys. It is of Old English origin and means 'victorious ship'. The name is most commonly used by English speakers.

Variant forms include: *Kellsey, Kellsie, Kelsea, Kelsee, Kelseigh, Kelsie* and *Kelsy.*

Kendall

This unisex name is more popular for boys than girls. It is of Old English origin and means 'the Kent River'. It refers to a river in Cumbria.

Variant forms include: *Kendal, Kendell* and *Kenny.*

Kendrick

The boy's name Kendrick is of Welsh origin and means 'great companion'. It may also mean 'royal power' or 'high hill'. The name *Kendra* is the female form of Kendrick.

Variant forms include: *Ken, Kendrix* and *Kenny.*

Kenneth

This boy's name is of Scottish and Celtic origin and means 'good looking, handsome one', or 'born of fire'. The name was adopted by English speakers in the mid-nineteenth century.

Variant forms include: *Ken, Kennith* and *Kenny*.

Kent

This boy's name, which is also a place name for a county in England, is of Old English origin and means 'edge or border'. The name was adopted as a first name in the mid-twentieth century.

Kerensa

This uncommon girl's name is rarely used outside Cornwall, a county in England. It is of Cornish origin and means 'love' or 'one who is full of love'.

Kerry

This unisex name is of Irish and Gaelic origin and means 'black'. The name is also derived from the Irish county of Kerry. It probably originated around the start of the twentieth century.

Variant forms include: *Kara, Kere* and *Kerrin*.

Top Ten Names After Saints

GIRLS	BOYS
MARY	NICHOLAS
ANNE	JUDE
ELIZABETH	PETER
CATHERINE	CHRISTOPHER
AGNES	LUKE

Kevin

The fairly popular boy's name Kevin is of Irish and Gaelic origin and means 'handsome beloved'. It also means 'gentle and kind'. The seventh-century Saint Kevin of Glendalough is the patron saint of Dublin.

Variant forms include: *Kevan* and *Kevon.*

Kian

The boy's name Kian is a variant form of the Irish and Gaelic *Cian*, and the Irish *Keon*, and means 'ancient one'. The name's history dates back to the second century.

Kiara

The girl's name Kiara is a variant of the Irish girl's name *Ciara*, which means 'little dark-haired one'. It can also mean 'one who is clever, famous and bright'.

Variant forms include: *Keira, Kiarra* and *Kierra.*

Kieran

The boy's name Kieran is of Irish and Gaelic origin and means 'dark-haired one'. It was the name of a sixth-century saint remembered for his generosity. *Ciara* is the female equivalent.

Variant forms include: *Ciaran* and *Kiran.*

Kim

This unisex name is now more common for girls than for boys. It is of Old English origin and means 'brave'. It may also refer to a 'field'. It is also a shortened form of the girl's name *Kimberley*.

Variant forms include: *Kimm, Kimme, Kimmie, Kimmy, Kimy, Kym* and *Kymme.*

Kimberley

This girl's name is of Old English origin and means 'royal field or forest clearing'. It was also derived from the name of the South African town of Kimberley.

Variant forms include: *Kim, Kimberly, Kimmie, Kimmy* and *Kym.*

King

This boy's name is a title name of Old English origin and growing in popularity among English speakers. It is a variant form of *Kingston* and *Kingsley* and means 'from the king's estate' or 'one from the royal meadow'. It may have been inspired by Martin Luther King, Jr (1929-68) or by Elvis Presley (1935-77), known as 'The King' (of rock and roll).

Kingsley

This boy's name is of Old English origin and means 'one from the royal meadow'. Today Kingsley is an unusual name for boys.

Variant forms include: *Kinsey, Kinslea, Kinslee, Kinsley, Kinslie* and *Kinsly*.

Kingston

The boy's name Kingston is of Old English origin and mainly used today by English speakers. It means 'from the king's estate' or 'one from the royal meadow'.

Kirk

The boy's name Kirk is of Old German and Old Norse origin and means 'church'. The name shot to prominence with the popularity of American actor Kirk Douglas (b.1916).

Variant forms include: *Kirke, Kirklan* and *Kirklyn*.

Kirsten

This girl's name is of Scandinavian origin and a variant of the Greek girl's name *Christine*, meaning 'Christian woman'. American actress Kirsten Dunst (b.1982) is a famous bearer of the name.

Variant forms include: *Kirstin* and *Kirsty*.

Kirsty

The girl's name Kirsty is of Scottish and Latin origin. It is a short form of *Kristine*, which is a variant of the Greek name *Christine* meaning 'a Christian woman'.

Variant forms include: *Christy* and *Kirstin*.

Kitty

The girl's name Kitty is a nickname or pet name for the Ancient Greek name *Katherine*, which means 'pure'. It developed as an independent name sometime during the sixteenth century.

Kyle

The boy's name Kyle is of Celtic origin and means 'straight, slender and narrow'. It is sometimes used as a girl's name, but is a more popular choice for boys.

Variant forms include: *Kile, Kiley, Kye* and *Kylan*.

Kylie

The girl's name Kylie is of English, Australian and Irish origin. It means 'boomerang' and 'graceful'. Australian pop singer Kylie Minogue (b.1968) is a famous bearer of the name.

Variant forms include: *Kiley, Kyla, Kylah, Kylea, Kylee, Kylene* and *Kyley*.

Top Ten Names Beginning with K

GIRLS	BOYS
KATIE	KYLE
KEIRA	KAI
KAYLA	KIAN
KYLIE	KAYDEN
KIRSTY	KIERAN

Lacey

This unisex name, although it is more common for girls, is of Old French origin and is a Norman place name. The name may also be influenced by the English word for 'lace'.

Variant forms include: *Lacie* and *Lacy*.

Lambert

This boy's name is of German and Scandinavian origin and means 'famous land'. The name was borne by Saint Lambert (636-700), Bishop of Maastricht, and came with the Normans to England.

Variant forms include: *Bert, Lambart* and *Landbert*.

Lance

The boy's name Lance is of Old French and German origin and means 'land'. It was also associated with the word 'lance', and in modern use is a nickname for the now uncommon name *Lancelot*.

Lara

The girl's name Lara is of Ancient Greek and Latin origin and means 'protection' as well as 'cheerful'. The name has become well known in recent times through Lara Croft, the action heroine of the *Tomb Raider* video game series (1996 - present) and movies (2001, 2003).

Variant forms include: *Larina, Larinda, Larita* and *Larra*.

Laura

The girl's name Laura is of Latin origin and means 'laurel plant or bay'. The love poems addressed to 'Laura' by the Italian poet Petrarch (1304-74) popularised the name in the Middle Ages and it has remained popular and widely used ever since.

Variant forms include: *Laurel, Laurie, Lora, Loren, Lorena, Lorene, Loretta, Lori, Lorie, Lorinda, Lorita, Lorna, Lorrie, Lorry* and *Lory*.

Lauren

This unisex name is a popular variant of the girl's name *Laura*, which means 'laurel plant or bay'. The name was made famous by American actress Lauren Bacall (b.1924) in the 1940s.

Lawrence

This boy's name is of Latin origin and means 'from Laurentum', a city south of Rome, which took its name from its laurel trees, perhaps in reference to a crown of laurel leaves.

Variant forms include: *Larry, Lars, Laurance, Lauren, Laurence, Lawrance, Lorance, Lorant, Loren, Lorence, Lorenz, Lorrence, Lorrenz, Lorry* and *Lowrance.*

Layla

This girl's name is a variant of *Leila* and *Lila* and means 'intoxication and beauty of the night'. For English speakers the name shot to prominence with Eric Clapton's love song 'Layla' (1970).

Leah

This girl's name is of Hebrew origin and means 'one who is delicate'. In the Old Testament Leah is Jacob's first wife. In modern times the variant form *Leia* has been made famous by the princess in the *Star Wars* films (1977-2008).

Variant forms include: *Lea, Lee, Leigh* and *Lia.*

Lee

This unisex name is of Old English origin and means 'meadow'. In the USA it was made famous and adopted in honour of the Confederate General Robert E. Lee (1807-70).

Variant forms include: *Leah* and *Lia.*

Leighton

This unusual boy's name is of Old English origin and means 'one from the settlement or meadow farm'. The use of the name peaked in the early twentieth century before declining in popularity.

Variant forms include: *Layton* and *Leyton.*

Top Ten Biblical Names

GIRLS	BOYS
EVE	LUKE
MARY	MATTHEW
RUTH	JOHN
REBECCA	MARK
NAOMI	JOSHUA

Leila

The exotic-sounding girl's name Leila is of Arabic origin and means 'night beauty'. It may also be derived from the word 'layla', which means 'intoxication and wine'.

Variant forms include: *Laila, Layla, Leela, Leelah, Leilah, Lela, Lelah, Lelia, Leyla, Lila, Lilah* and *Lyla*.

Lena

The origin of this name is debated, as it could have developed as a shortened form of *Marlene, Eileen* and *Helen*, but it may also be of Latin origin with the meaning of 'one who is alluring'.

Variant forms include: *Leena, Leina, Leyna* and *Lina*.

Lennon

This boy's name is of Gaelic origin and means 'little cloak'. The popularisation of the name is, however, more likely in homage to English songwriting legend John Lennon (1940-80) of The Beatles.

Leo

This boy's name is of Latin origin and means 'lion'. It was a very popular name in Roman times, no doubt because of its association with a lion-hearted, strong personality.

Variant forms include: *Lee, Leon* and *Lyon*.

Leon

This boy's name is a popular variant of the name *Leo*, which simply means 'lion' and, by association, all the qualities that a lion symbolises, such as strength and grandeur.

Leonard

This boy's name is of Old German origin and means 'strength of the lion'. Often shortened to the less formal *Leo*, it is associated with the Italian Renaissance artist and scientist Leonardo da Vinci (1452-1519).

Variant forms include: *Lee, Len, Lennie, Lenny, Leo, Leon* and *Leonardo*.

Leonora

This girl's name is of Greek origin and means 'bright one, shining one and compassion'. Various forms of the name have been popular in literature, for example, in Edgar Allan Poe's poem 'Lenore' (1843).

Variant forms include: *Leanora, Leanore, Lenora, Lenore, Leonor, Leonore*.

Leslie

This unisex name, although it tends to be more popular for girls, is of Scottish and Gaelic origin and means 'garden of hollies'. It was first used as a given name in the eighteenth century.

Variant forms include: *Lesley, Lesly, Lezlee, Lezley* and *Lezlie*.

Lester

This fairly uncommon boy's name is of Old English origin and is a place name, meaning 'man from Leicester'. It may also derive from words that mean 'Roman fort'.

Letitia

This girl's name is of Latin origin and means 'joyful happiness'. The original form of the name, *Laetitia*, was first used by English speakers in the Middle Ages.

Variant forms include: *Latisha, Leticia, Lettice, Lettie, Lettitia, Letty, Tish* and *Tisha*.

Lewis

This boy's name is of English origin. It is a variant of the Old German, *Louis*, which means 'famous fighter'. The author of *Alice's Adventures in Wonderland*, Lewis Carroll (1832-98), is a famous bearer of the name.

Lexi

This girl's name is a pet form, which has become an independent name, of the Greek names *Alexandra* and *Alexis*, and means 'one who is defender and protector'.

Lexie is a variant form.

Top Ten Names in Germany

GIRLS	BOYS
ANNA	LUCAS
LEONIE	LEON
LEAH	LUCA
LENA	TIM
HANNA	PAUL

Liam

This boy's name is of Old German origin and means 'helmet and protection'. Irish actor Liam Neeson (b.1952) is a famous bearer of the name. It is also a shortened form of *William*.

Lyam is a variant form.

Libby

The girl's name Libby is of English origin and a popular pet form, which has become an independent name, of the Hebrew girl's name *Elizabeth*, which means 'God's promise'.

Variant forms include: *Lib, Libbee, Libbey, Libbie, Libet* and *Liby*.

Liberty

The girl's name Liberty is of English origin and it is derived from the words 'freedom and liberty'. Since the 2000s the popularity of this name has gradually been rising.

Lila

This girl's name is of Arabic origin and means 'intoxication and night beauty'. It also refers to the colour lilac and is a shortened form of the Hebrew girl's name *Delilah*, meaning 'seductive'.

Variant forms include: *Layla, Leela, Leila, Lilah, Lyla* and *Lylah*.

Lillian

This girl's name is of Latin origin and is a flower name meaning 'lily'. The name could also have evolved from a combination of the names *Lily* and *Anne*.

Variant forms include: *Lila, Lilian, Liliana, Liliane, Lilianna, Lillie, Lilly, Lillyan* and *Lillyanne*.

Lily

This girl's name is of Latin origin and means 'lily', a flower that is an age-old symbol of beauty, purity and innocence. It is also a variant form of *Elizabeth*.

Variant forms include: *Lila, Lili, Lilia, Lilian, Liliana, Liliane, Lilla, Lilley, Lilli, Lillia, Lillianne, Lilly, Lilyan* and *Lilyanne*.

Linda

This girl's name is of Spanish origin and means 'pretty'. Other derivations suggest that it may also mean 'gentle and friendly and kind'. It is also a pet form for *Belinda* and *Melinda*.

Variant forms include: *Lin, Lindee, Lindey, Lindi, Lindie, Lindira, Lindka, Lindy, Linn, Lyn, Lynda, Lynn* and *Lynne*.

Lindford

The boy's name Lindford is of Old English origin and means 'linden tree ford'. British track athlete Linford Christie (b.1960) is a famous bearer of the name.

Variant forms include: *Linford, Linnford* and *Lynford*.

Lindsay

This unisex name, which is now more common as a girl's name, is of Old English origin and means 'island of linden trees'. In Scotland it is still used as a boy's name.

Variant forms include: *Lindsey* and *Lyndsey*.

Lionel

This boy's name is of Latin origin and means 'young lion', an age-old symbol of strength, courage, potential and grandeur. It is also a variant form of *Leo* and *Leon*.

Linus

This boy's name is of Greek origin and means 'flax'. In Greek mythology Linus is the musical son of Apollo. Linus was also known as the personification of a ritual refrain or lamentation.

Lisa

The girl's name Lisa is of English origin and a popular variant form, which has become an independent name, of the Hebrew girl's name *Elizabeth*, which means 'God's promise'. The sixteenth-century painting 'Mona Lisa' is a portrait of Lisa del Giocondo (1479-1542/1551) by Leonardo da Vinci.

Variant forms include: *Leesa, Leeza, Lise, Lisebet,* and *Liza*.

Liv

The girl's name Liv is of Old Norse and Latin origin and means 'defend and protect'. Modern use links it to the Norwegian word for 'life'. It is also a shortened form for *Olivia*.

Lloyd

This boy's name is of Welsh origin and means 'sacred and grey-haired', it therefore suggests wisdom, authority and experience of life. It is also a form of the boy's name *Floyd*.

Logan

The unisex name Logan is of Gaelic origin and means 'little hollow'. It is mostly used as a boy's name in Scotland and *Logen* is the only variant form.

Lola

This girl's name is a shortened form of the Spanish name *Dolores*, which means 'sorrow'. It is also a pet form of *Laura* and *Lourdes*.
   Variant forms include: *Lolita* and *Lolla*.

Top Ten Names after Rock and Pop Stars

GIRLS	BOYS
LEONA	ELVIS
CHERYL	LIAM
BEYONCÉ	JOHN
ALICIA	PAUL
KYLIE	ROBBIE

Lolita

This girl's name is a variant of *Lola* and means 'sorrow'. It is associated with sexual prematurity due to Vladimir Nabokov's 1955 novel, *Lolita*, about a young girl who had an older admirer.

Lorna

This girl's name is of Scottish origin and refers to a place called Lorn in Scotland. The name was made famous as the heroine in the nineteenth-century romantic novel *Lorna Doone* (1869) by Richard Doddridge Blackmore.

Lorraine

This girl's name is of French origin and means 'from Lorraine', a region in France. The name was adopted by English speakers in the late-nineteenth century.

Variant forms include: *Lorain, Loraina, Loraine, Lori, Lorine, Lorraina* and *Lorrayne.*

Louis

This boy's name is of Old German origin and means 'famous warrior'. Various forms of the name have been used by noble and royal families in France and Germany.

Variant forms include: *Louie, Lewis* and *Luis.*

Louise

This girl's name is the feminine form of the Old German *Louis*, which means 'famed warrior'. In the eighteenth and nineteenth centuries *Louisa* was a more common form of the name.

Variant forms include: *Aloisa, Aloise, Aloysia, Eloisa, Eloise, Lois, Loise, Lola, Lolita, Lou, Louisiana, Louisina, Lu, Luisa, Luise* and *Lulu.*

Lourdes

The girl's name Lourdes is of French origin and is a place name for Lourdes in France, where the Virgin *Mary* is said to have appeared in 1858 to Saint *Bernadette* (1844-79). In 1996 the American singer Madonna (b.1958) chose the name for her first daughter.

Luca

This boy's name is of Ancient Greek origin and means 'man from Lucania'. It is used predominately by Italian speakers, and is a variant of the widely used name *Luke*.

Lucas

This is a variant of the Latin boy's name *Luke*, which was introduced to England by the Normans in the eleventh century and means 'shining and white'. It is popular in Germany.

Variant forms include: *Loucas, Loukas* and *Lukas*.

Lucian

This boy's name is of Latin origin and means 'light, bright or born at daybreak'. In the Middle Ages the name was often given to boys born at daybreak.

Variant forms include: *Lucianus, Lucias* and *Lukyan*.

Luciana

The girl's name Luciana is a variant of the popular name *Lucy* and means 'first light'. It has its origins in the Latin language and could also be the feminine form of *Lucian*.

Lucille

This girl's name is of French origin and a variant of the Latin name *Lucy*, which means 'first light'. Its popularity was revived in the twentieth century by American comedienne Lucille Ball (1911-89).

Variant forms include: *Lucienne, Lucila, Lucile, Lucilia* and *Lucilla*.

Lucinda

This girl's name is a variant of the Latin name *Lucy*, which means 'first light'. Often borne by aristocrats, the name was first adopted by English speakers in the eighteenth century.

Variant forms include: *Cindy, Lucena, Lucina, Lucinna* and *Lusine.*

Lucy

This enduringly popular girl's name is of Latin origin and means 'light, bright or born at daybreak'. In the Middle Ages the name was often given to girls born at dawn.

Variant forms include: *Lou, Loulou, Lu, Luca, Lucetta, Lucette, Luci, Lucia, Luciana, Lucianna, Lucie, Lucienne, Lucile, Lucilla, Lucille, Lucina* and *Lucinda.*

Ludovic

This boy's name is of Old German origin and means 'famous and loud warrior'. In English a variant of this rarely used name is the shortened form *Ludo.*

Variant forms include: *Louis* and *Ludwig.*

Luke

The ever-popular boy's name Luke is of Greek origin and means 'one who is from Lucania', a region in southern Italy. Saint Luke is the patron saint of doctors and artists, and the first-century Christian who wrote one of the four gospels in the Bible. The name is also associated with the fictional Luke Skywalker, hero of the *Star Wars* films (1977–2008).

Variant forms include: *Luca, Lucas, Lucian, Lucius* and *Lukas.*

Lulu

This uncommon girl's name is of Swahili and Hawaiian origin, and means 'precious, gem, peaceful and protected'. It may also be a pet form of the girl's name *Louise.*

Lydia

This girl's name is of Greek origin and means 'woman from Lydia', an ancient region in Asia Minor, which is now in Turkey. The name was adopted by English speakers in the seventeenth century.

Variant forms include: *Lyda* and *Lydie.*

Lyndon

This unisex name, although it is more popular for boys, is of English origin and refers to a 'tall and graceful tree'. US President Lyndon Johnson, (1908-1973) was a famous bearer of the name.

Variant forms include: *Lindon* and *Linden*.

Lynette

This girl's name is of Old Welsh origin and means 'nymph' or 'idol or image'. Today the name is regarded as a variant of *Lynn* and has been associated with the linnet. The girls name *Llinos* is the Welsh for linnet.

Variant forms include: *Linett, Linette, Linnet, Lynett, Lynetta, Lynnet* and *Lynnette*.

Lynn

The girl's name Lynn is of Old English and Gaelic origin and means 'waterfall, lake or pool'. It may also be a variant of the Spanish *Linda*, meaning 'pretty'.

Variant forms include: *Lin, Linn, Lynette, Lynne, Lynnelle* and *Lynnett*.

Top Ten Names Beginning with L

GIRLS	BOYS
LILY	LEWIS
LUCY	LIAM
LEAH	LUKE
LOLA	LUCAS
LILLY	LEO

Madeline

This girl's name is of Hebrew origin and means 'woman from Magdala', a village on the Sea of Galilee, and the home of Mary Magdalene, a follower of Jesus, who is considered a saint by Roman Catholics.

Variant forms include: *Lynn, Madalene, Madalyn, Maddie, Maddy, Madelaine, Madeleine, Madelene, Madge, Magdala, Magdalena, Magdalene, Marlene* and *Maud*.

Madison

This unisex name is of Old English origin and means 'mighty warrior'. It may also mean 'son of *Maud*', or be a diminutive of *Madeline*. It is a more popular choice of name for girls than boys.

Variant forms include: *Maddie, Maddison, Maddy, Madisen* and *Madyson*.

Madonna

The girl's name Madonna is of Italian origin and means 'my lady', a form of respectful introduction. For Roman Catholics the name represents the Virgin Mary. In modern times the name has been famously linked to the controversial singer, dancer and actress Madonna (b.1958).

Variant forms include: *Donna* and *Madona*.

Maeve

This fairly rare girl's name outside of Ireland is of Irish origin and means 'intoxicating' or 'she who intoxicates'. *Mave* and *Mavis* (also meaning 'song thrush') are English variants.

Magnus

This boy's name is of Latin origin and means 'great'. It was first known from the Roman Emperor Charlemagne (c.747), whose name was recorded as 'Carolus Magnus' or 'Charles the Great'.

Variant forms include: *Magnes, Magnusson* and *Manus*.

Maia

This girl's name is of Greek origin and means 'great mother'. In Roman mythology Maia is the earth goddess of springtime, and in Greek mythology she is a beautiful nymph.

Variant forms include: *Mai, Maja, May, Maya, Mayah, Moia, Moja, Moya* and *Mya*.

Maisie

This girl's name is of Ancient Greek and English origin and is a nickname, which became an independent name, for *Margaret*, meaning 'pearl'. It may also be a variant of *Marjorie*.

Variant forms include: *Maisey, Maisy* and *Mazie*.

Malcolm

This boy's name is of Scottish and Gaelic origin and means 'a follower of Saint Columba'. Saint Columba (521-97) was a Gaelic missionary monk who converted many Scots to Christianity.

Variant forms include: *Malcom* and *Malkolm*.

Manfred

This rare boy's name is of Old German origin and means 'strong and great peace', or 'a man of peace'. *Freddy* is a more popular English variant of the name.

Variant forms include: *Manfrid, Manfried, Mannfred* and *Mannfryd*.

Marcia

This girl's name is the feminine form of *Marcus*. It is of Latin origin and means 'devoted to or dedicated to Mars'. Mars was the Roman god of war.

Variant forms include: *Marcella, Marcene, Marci, Marcie, Marcila, Marcile, Marcille, Marcine, Marcy* and *Marsha*.

Marcus

This boy's name is of Latin origin and means 'war-like or devoted to Mars'. Mars was the Roman god of war and springtime, after whom the month of March was named.

Variant forms include: *Marcas, Marco, Markos* and *Markus.*

Margaret

This widely used girl's name is of Ancient Greek origin and means 'pearl'. It was first known in Scotland from Saint Margaret of Scotland (1045-93), who married Malcolm III, King of Scots, and by the end of the eleventh century the name had spread to other English-speaking countries.

Variant forms include: *Madge, Mag, Maggi, Maggie, Maggy, Maisie, Maisy, Margareta, Margarete, Margaretta, Margarita, Margarite, Margaruite, Marge, Margeret, Margeretta, Margery, Marget, Margo, Margot, Marjorey, Marjorie, Marjory, Meg, Megan, Meggie, Meggy, Peg, Peggie* and *Peggy.*

Margot

Like *Margo*, this girl's name is a French variant of the Greek name *Margaret*, which means 'pearl'. It was made famous by English ballerina Margot Fonteyn (1919-91).

Maria

This girl's name is of Hebrew and Latin origin. The meaning is disputed, with some sources suggesting it means 'bitterness' and others infer it means 'my beloved', or 'star of the sea'.

Variant forms include: *Mariah, Marie, Marieanne, Mia* and *Moriah.*

Mariah

This girl's name is a popular variant of *Maria* and *Mary* and means 'drop or star of the sea'. American singer, songwriter and actress Mariah Carey (b.1970) is a famous bearer of the name.

Marian

This girl's name is of Hebrew and French origin and a blend of the Latin name *Mary*, meaning 'star of the sea', and the Hebrew name *Ann*, meaning 'grace'.

Variant forms include: *Mariam, Mariana, Mariane, Marion, Maryann* and *Maryanne.*

Marianne

This girl's name was adopted by English speakers in the eighteenth century and blends the Christian names of the Virgin Mary, which means 'star of the sea', and her mother *Ann*, which means 'grace'.

Variant forms include: *Marianda, Mariane, Mariann, Marianna, Marien, Maryam, Maryan, Maryann* and *Maryanna.*

Marie

This girl's name is of Hebrew origin and a French variant of the Latin *Mary*, which means 'my beloved', or 'star of the sea'. Scientist Marie Curie (1867-1934) was a famous bearer of the name.

Top Ten Names Associated with Influential People

GIRLS	BOYS
MARGARET	DAVID
DIANA	HARRY
CHERYL	SIMON
HELEN	JOHN
KELLY	MICHAEL

Marilyn

This girl's name is of English origin and a modern blend of *Mary*, meaning 'star of the sea', and *Lynn*, meaning, 'lake, waterfall or pool'. American sex symbol Marilyn Monroe (1926-62) was a famous bearer of the name.

Variant forms include: *Maralyn, Marilin, Marillyn, Marilynn, Marrilin, Marrilyn, Marylin, Marylyn* and *Marylynn*.

Mario

This boy's name is of Latin origin and means 'manly, male'. It may also be a variant of *Marius*, also meaning 'virile, dedicated to Mars', and the boy's name *Mark*.

Marion

This unisex name, although today it is more common for girls, is of French origin and a variant of the Latin girl's name *Mary*, meaning 'star of the sea'.

Variant forms include: *Marian, Maryon* and *Maryonn*.

Marjorie

The girl's name Marjorie is of English origin and a variant of the French name *Margery*, which in turn is a variant of the Greek name *Margaret*, meaning 'pearl'.

Mark

The boy's name Mark is a widely used variant of the Latin name *Marcus*, meaning 'war-like' or 'dedicated to Mars'. The name was borne by one of the evangelists who wrote the second gospel in the New Testament, which is named after him.

Variant forms include: *Marc, Marco, Marcos, Marcus, Mario, Marius, Marko, Markos* and *Marquus*.

Marlene

This girl's name is of Old German origin and is a combination of the Latin, *Maria*, and the Greek, *Magdalene*. The German-born actress Marlene Dietrich (1901-92), was a famous bearer of the name.

Variant forms include: *Marla, Marleen, Marleena, Marleene, Marleina, Marna* and *Marline*.

Marlon

The boy's name Marlon is of English origin and means 'little hawk'. It is also a variant of the rarely used Celtic name *Merlin*, which means 'fortress'. Actor Marlon Brando (1924-2004) was a famous bearer of the name.

Martha

This girl's name is of Aramaic origin and means 'lady of the house'. In the Bible, Martha busied herself with housework while her sister, Mary of Bethany, listened to Jesus.

Variant forms include: *Marla, Marleen, Marleena, Marleene, Marley, Marlie, Marlin, Marlina, Marline, Marlyn, Marlynne, Martina* and *Marna*.

Martin

The widely used boy's name Martin is of Latin origin and means 'dedicated to Mars'. Mars was the Roman god of war. Civil rights activist, Martin Luther King (1929-68) was a famous bearer of the name.

Variant forms include: *Marten, Marti, Martie, Marton, Marty, Martyn* and *Morten*.

Martina

The girl's name Martina is the feminine form of *Martin*. Tennis champions, Martina Navratilova (b.1956) and Martina Hingis (b.1980) are famous bearers of this name.

Variant forms include: *Marta, Marteena, Martie, Martine, Marty* and *Tina*.

Mary

This widely used girl's name is of Latin, Greek and Hebrew origin and means 'my beloved'. Other possible meanings include 'star of the sea', 'sea of bitterness', and 'much longed-for child'. The name was borne by several women in the Bible, most notably the Virgin *Mary*, mother of Jesus.

Variant forms include: *Maria, Mariam, Marion, Marla, Maryann, Maryanne, Maureen, Minnie, Moira, Mollie, Molly, Morag, Moya* and *Muriel*.

Maryam

This girl's name is a variant of the name *Marianne*, which means 'grace' and 'star of the sea', and *Miriam*, which is an ancient version of the name *Mary*.

Mason

This boy's name is of English and French origin and means 'mason, stone worker' or 'one who works with stone'. Since the 1950s, the name has been steadily increasing in popularity.

Matilda

This girl's name is of Old German origin and means 'one who is mighty in battle'. The name was brought to England in the eleventh century by William the Conqueror's queen, Matilda.

Variant forms include: *Mattie, Matty, Maud, Maude, Tilda, Tillie* and *Tilly*.

Matthew

This widely used boy's name is of Hebrew origin and means 'gift from God'. In the Bible it is the name of the apostle who wrote the first gospel, and bears his name.

Variant forms include: *Mat, Mathew, Matt, Mattheus, Matthias, Mattie, Matty* and *Matz*.

Maureen

The girl's name Maureen is of Irish and Gaelic origin and means 'a star of the sea'. It is a form of the widely used name *Mary*, with some sources suggesting it means 'little Mary'.

Variant forms include: *Mo, Moira, Mora, Moreen, Morena, Morene* and *Moria*.

Max

This boy's name is a shortened form of *Maximilian*, or *Maxwell*, that emerged as an independent name in the late-nineteenth century. It can also be a shortened form for the girl's name *Maxine*.

Top Ten Names in Northern Ireland

GIRLS	BOYS
KATIE	JACK
GRACE	JAMES
SOPHIE	MATTHEW
LUCY	DANIEL
EMMA	RYAN

Maximilian

This boy's name is of Latin origin and means 'the greatest'. Adopted by English speakers at the start of the seventeenth century, by the end of the nineteenth century it was overtaken in popularity by the shortened form *Max*.

Variant forms include: *Mac, Mack, Maks, Maxey, Maxemilian, Maxemilion, Maxie, Maximilien, Maximillian, Maximino, Maximo, Maximos* and *Maxy*.

Maxine

This girl's name is of Latin origin and in the early part of the twentieth century it developed as the feminine form of *Max* and *Maximilian*, which mean 'the greatest'.

Variant forms include: *Maxeen, Maxi, Maxie, Maxime* and *Maxy*.

Maxwell

This boy's name is an Old English and Scottish name and means 'from Mack's stream or pool'. It may also have been derived from the Latin name *Magnus*, which means 'great'.

Variant forms include: *Mack, Max, Maxie* and *Maxy*.

May

This girl's name is of English origin and it refers to the fifth month of the year, May. It may also refer to a Sanskrit word that means 'dream or illusion'.

Variant forms include: *Mae, Maia, Mala, Maya* and *Maye.*

Maya

This girl's name is of Spanish, Hindi and Russian origin. It means 'a dream or illusion' and may also be a variant of the Latin *Maia*, meaning 'great mother'.

Variant forms include: *Maiya, Miah* and *Miya.*

Megan

This girl's name is of Welsh origin and a variant of the girl's name *Margaret*, which means 'pearl'. It is often shortened to *Meg*, which is also an independent name.

Variant forms include: *Meagan, Meaghan, Megen, Meggie, Meggy* and *Meghan.*

Melanie

This girl's name, often shortened to *Mel*, is of Ancient Greek origin and means 'black or dark skinned'. It was originally given to children with black or dark complexion, hair and eyes.

Variant forms include: *Melaney, Melani, Melanney, Melannie, Melany, Melly, Meloni* and *Melonie.*

Melissa

This girl's name is of Ancient Greek origin and means 'honeybee'. In Greek mythology the name was borne by a nymph who saved and fed Zeus and was turned into a honeybee.

Variant forms include: *Lisa, Mel, Melesa, Melessa, Melicent, Mellisa, Melly, Millicent, Millie,* and *Missie.*

Melvin

This boy's name, often shortened to *Mel*, is probably of Irish and Gaelic origin and it has a number of meanings including 'smooth brow', 'chief' and 'friend of the sword'.

Variant forms include: *Melvon, Melvyn, Melwyn* and *Vinnie*.

Meredith

This unisex name, although it is far more popular for girls, is of Welsh origin and means 'great chief or ruler'. It may also mean 'protector of the sea'.

Variant forms include: *Meradith, Meredithe, Meredyth, Meridith, Merridie* and *Merry*.

Mervyn

This boy's name is of Welsh origin and means 'friend of the sea'. It was the name of a ninth-century Welsh king. It may also mean 'sea hill'.

Variant forms include: *Marlin, Merlin* and *Mervin*.

Meryl

This girl's name, a variant of *Muriel*, is of Old English origin and means 'shining sea'. Oscar-winning, American actress Meryl Streep (b.1949) is a famous bearer of the name.

Variant forms include: *Merla, Merrell, Merril, Merryl, Meryle* and *Meryll*.

Mia

This girl's name is of Latin, Scandinavian and Israeli origin and is a feminine form of *Michael*, and a variant form of *Mary* and *Maria*.

Variant forms include: *Mea* and *Meya*.

Michael

This boy's name, which has a large number of variant forms, is of Hebrew origin and means 'he who resembles or is much like God'. Through the centuries this widely used name has been borne by an archangel, as well as saints, emperors and kings. It is often shortened to the pet forms *Mike* or *Mick*.

Variant forms include: *Micael, Micah, Mical, Micha, Michail, Michal, Micheal, Michel, Michelangelo, Michele, Mickey, Micky, Miguel, Mike, Mikkel, Miquel, Mitch, Mitchell, Mychael, Mychal* and *Mykell*.

Michaela

This girl's name is a popular variant of the Hebrew girl's name *Michelle*, which means 'who is like God'. Some sources suggest it could also be of Gaelic origin and mean 'fiery nature'.

Michelle

This popular girl's name, which is often shortened to the pet form *Shell*, is of Hebrew origin and means 'who resembles or is like God'. It is the feminine form of *Michael*.

Variant forms include: *Michaela, Michele, Mikaela, Miquela, Mychele, Mychelle, Myshell* and *Myshella*.

Miles

This boy's name is of Old German origin and means 'generous and merciful'. It could also be a variant of the Latin name *Emil*, which means 'keen to please'.

Variant forms include: *Milan, Milo, Myles* and *Mylo*.

Miley

This unisex name is of German origin and means 'generous and merciful'. American singer and actress Miley Cyrus (b.1992) of the *Hannah Montana* American TV series (2006–present) fame, is a well-known bearer of the name.

Variant forms include: *Milea, Milee, Milie* and *Mily*.

Millie

This girl's name, which also appears as *Milly*, is a variant of several names, including *Amelia, Camilla, Emily, Mary* and *Melissa*. It means 'hardworking, honeybee, and strength'.

Mimi

This girl's name is of French origin and a pet name for *Maria, Mira* and *Miriam*. It first appeared as an independent name after Puccini's opera *La bohème* (1896), with its tragic heroine Mimi.

Miranda

This girl's name is of Latin origin and means 'worthy of respect and admiration'. Adopted by English speakers in the mid-nineteenth century, it also means 'wonderful and adorable'.

Variant forms include: *Mira, Miran, Mirandah, Mirranda, Myra* and *Myranda.*

Miriam

This girl's name is of Hebrew origin and is an ancient version of the name Mary. In the Bible Miriam is the sister of Moses, who saved his life as a baby.

Variant forms include: *Mariam, Mimi, Mirham, Mirriam, Miryam* and *Myriam.*

Misty

This unusual girl's name is of English origin and simply means 'mist'. It was first adopted after the film *Play Misty For Me* (1971), directed by and starring Clint Eastwood.

Variant forms include: *Misti, Mistie, Mystee* and *Mysti.*

Mohammad

This boy's name is a widely used variant of the Arabic name *Muhammad*, which means 'worthy of praise'. It is the name of the sacred founder and prophet of Islam.

Mohammed

This boy's name is a widely used variant of the Arabic name *Muhammad*, which means 'worthy of praise'. It is the name of the sacred founder and prophet of Islam.

Moira

This girl's name is of English origin and a variant of *Mary*, meaning 'star of the sea', or 'my beloved'. It has been adopted by English speakers, especially in Scotland, since the nineteenth century.

Moyra is a variant form.

Molly

This girl's name is of Irish origin and a variant of *Mary*, which means 'star of the sea'. Well known in Ireland from the song 'Molly Malone', which was based on a beautiful, seventeenth-century street hawker in Dublin.

Variant forms include: *Moll, Mollee, Molley, Molli* and *Mollie*.

Mona

This girl's name is of Irish origin and means 'noble'. Mona is also a shortened form of *Madonna*, and the artist's model for the 'Mona Lisa' (started in 1503/4), painted by Leonardo da Vinci, bore this name.

Variant forms include: *Monah, Monalisa, Monalissa, Monna* and *Moyna*.

Monica

This girl's name is of Latin and Greek origin and means 'solitary', and 'to warn and advise'. The name was borne by Saint Monica of Hippo (332-387). She was the mother of Saint Augustine and guided him to Christianity.

Variant forms include: *Mona, Monicka, Monika, Monike, Monique* and *Monnica*.

Montgomery

This uncommon boy's name is of Old French and German origin and means 'power of men' or 'hill of the powerful one'. American actor Montgomery Clift (1920-66) is a famous bearer of the name.

Variant forms: *Monte, Montgomerie, Montie* and *Monty*.

Morag

This unisex name, although it is more common for girls, is of Celtic origin and means 'big and great. It could also be a variant of *Mary*, which means 'star of the sea'.

Morgan

This unisex name is of Welsh and Old English origin and means 'born bright' or 'circling sea'. In Arthurian legend Morgan le Fay is a powerful and dangerous sorceress.

Variant forms include: *Morgaine, Morgana, Morgayne, Morgen* and *Morgin*.

Morton

This boy's name is of Old English origin and means 'moor town or settlement'. Possibly a variant of *Moses*, it was first used by English speakers in the mid-nineteenth century.

Morten is a variant form.

Moses

The boy's name Moses is of Hebrew and Egyptian origin and means 'child' and 'saviour'. In the Old Testament Moses is the great leader of the exiled Israelites.

Variant forms include: *Moss, Moyses* and *Mozes*.

Muhammad

This widely used boy's name is of Arabic origin and means 'praiseworthy', or 'to praise, to commend, and to thank'. It is the name of the sacred founder and Prophet of Islam and, as a result, is a very popular name within Muslim communities.

Variant forms include: *Hamid, Hammad, Mohamad, Mohamed, Mohamet, Mohammad, Mohammed, Muhamet* and *Muhammed*.

Muriel

This girl's name is of Irish and Gaelic origin. It means 'sea bright', or 'shining, sparkling sea'. It dates back to the Middle Ages and may be a variant form of *Meryl* and *Mary*.

Variant forms include: *Murial, Muriella* and *Murielle*.

Murray

This boy's name is of Irish and Gaelic origin and means 'settlement by the sea' and 'master and lord of the sea'. Today Murray is an uncommon boy's name.

Variant forms include: *Moray, Murrey* and *Murry*.

Murron

This unusual girl's name is of Scottish and Celtic origin and is a variant of the Irish name *Muireann*, which means 'white and fair' and 'sea'. Murron is sometimes confused with *Maureen*.

Mya

This girl's name is a variant of the Greek name *Maia*, which means 'great mother', and the Latin name *Maya*, meaning 'a dream or illusion'. In Burmese its meaning is 'emerald'.

Top Ten Names Beginning with M

GIRLS	BOYS
MIA	MOHAMMED
MEGAN	MATTHEW
MILLIE	MUHAMMED
MOLLY	MICHAEL
MATILDA	MASON

Nadia

This girl's name is of Russian origin and means 'hope'. It is a very popular girl's name in Russia. Romanian gymnast Nadia Comaneci (b.1961) is a famous bearer of the name.

Nancy

The origin of this girl's name is uncertain. It could be a variant of the Hebrew girl's name *Ann*, which means 'grace'. It is well known today through the teenage detective in the *Nancy Drew* mystery series of books (1930 - present).

Variant forms include: *Nance, Nancee, Nancey, Nanci, Nancie, Nann, Nanny, Nansee* and *Nansey*.

Nanette

The girl's name Nanette is of French origin and probably a variant of the Hebrew girl's name *Ann*, which means 'one who has been graced with God's favour'.

Variant forms include: *Nan, Nancy* and *Ninette*.

Naomi

This girl's name is of Hebrew origin and means 'pleasant'. It may also mean 'sweet' and 'my delight'. Although a traditional Jewish name, it is widely used outside Jewish communities.

Variant forms include: *Naomie, Nayomi, Neoma, Neomi, Noami, Noemi* and *Noemie*.

Natalie

This girl's name is of Latin origin and means 'birthday', referring to the birth of Christ at Christmas time. In Russia the name is often given to girls born in the Christmas season.

Variant forms include: *Nat, Nata, Natala, Natale, Natalee, Natalia, Natalina, Nataline, Natalja, Natallia, Natallie, Natalya, Natasha, Nathalia* and *Nathalie*.

Natasha

This girl's name is of Latin origin and means 'birthday', referring to the birth of Christ or Christmas time. The name is often shortened to the pet form *Tasha*.

Variant forms include: *Nataasha, Natalie, Natascha, Natashah, Natashia, Natashja, Tash, Tashia, Tashie, Tosha* and *Toshia*.

Nathan

This boy's name is of Hebrew origin and means 'God has given' or 'gift from God'. It is also a shortened form that has become an independent of the names *Nathaniel* and *Jonathan*.

Variant forms include: *Nat, Nathen* and *Nathon*.

Nathaniel

This uncommon boy's name is of Hebrew origin and means 'God has given'. The name's popularity was boosted by the Sir Nathaniel character in Shakespeare's comedy *Love's Labour's Lost* (written in 1595 or 1596).

Variant forms include: *Nathan* and *Nathanial*.

Neil

The boy's name Neil is of Latin, Irish and Gaelic origin and means 'champion'. Some disputed sources suggest it may also mean 'passion', 'war horn' and 'cloud'.

Variant forms include: *Neal, Neel, Neill, Neille, Nial, Niall, Niel, Nile* and *Niles*.

Nell

This girl's name is a variant of the Latin name *Cornelia*, the Greek names *Eleanor* and *Helen*, and the English name *Nelly* or *Nellie*, and means, 'war horn, sunlight' and 'God is my light'. Eleanor 'Nell' Gwyn (1650-87) was the adored mistress of Charles II (1630-85).

Nelson

This boy's name is a variant of *Neil*, which means 'champion'. It may also mean 'son of Neil' and was first bestowed in honour of the British Admiral Lord Nelson (1758-1805).

Variant forms include: *Neilson, Nelsen, Niles* and *Nilsson*.

Top Ten Names in Scotland

GIRLS	BOYS
SOPHIE	JACK
OLIVIA	LEWIS
AVA	LIAM
EMILY	LOGAN
LUCY	JAMES

Nerissa

The girl's name Nerissa or *Narissa* is of Greek or Italian origin and means 'sea nymph', or 'dark-haired one'. It was invented by Shakespeare for a female character in *The Merchant of Venice* (written between 1596 and 1598).

Nerys

This girl's name is of Ancient Greek and Welsh origin and means 'noblewoman'. It may also mean 'white lady'. The name is rarely used outside Wales.

Variant forms include: *Neris, Neriss* and *Neryss*.

Nestor

The uncommon boy's name Nestor or *Nester*, which was borne by several early saints, is of Greek origin and means 'homecoming', 'he who remembers' and 'traveller'.

Neville

This boy's name is of Old French origin and means 'one who is from the new village or town'. Today Neville is not a common name.

Variant forms include: *Nev, Nevil, Nevile, Nevill* and *Nevyle*.

Nia

The girl's name Nia is of Gaelic and Swahili origin and means 'aim, purpose and goal'. Some sources suggest it may also mean 'cloud, passion, beauty and radiance'.

Variant forms include: *Nea, Niah, Nya* and *Nyah.*

Niamh

The girl's name Niamh (pronounced NIY-V) is of Celtic origin and means 'shining and radiant beauty'. In Irish mythology the name was borne by the sea god's daughter.

Variant forms include: *Neev, Neve, Nia, Niah* and *Niam.*

Nicholas

The widely used boy's name Nicholas, which is frequently shortened to the pet name *Nick*, is of Ancient Greek origin and means 'victory to the people'. The name was borne by Saint Nicholas (270-343), Bishop of Myra, who was believed to give presents secretly to others, and later became known as Santa Claus.

Variant forms include: *Nic, Nicklas, Nickolas, Nicky, Nicolas, Niklas, Niklos, Nikolai, Nikolas, Nikolaus, Nikolay, Nikolos, Nikos, Nilos* and *Nils.*

Nicola

This widely used girl's name is of Ancient Greek origin and means 'victory to the people'. The feminine version of *Nicholas*, it has been in use among English speakers since the twelfth century.

Variant forms include: *Niccola, Nichola, Nickola* and *Nikola.*

Nicole

This girl's name is a variant of *Nicola*. It is of Ancient Greek origin and means 'victory to the people'. *Nicolette* is a popular French variant of the name.

Variant forms include: *Nic, Niccole, Nichol, Nichole, Nicholle, Nicolina* and *Nikole*.

Nigel

The boy's name Nigel is of Gaelic origin and means 'champion'. It is a variant of *Niall* and *Neil* and may also mean 'cloud' and 'passionate'. *Nigella* is the female equivalent.

Nigella

This girl's name is the feminine form of *Nigel* and means 'champion', 'passionate' and 'cloud'. The British food writer and journalist Nigella Lawson (b.1960) is a well-known bearer of the name.

Nikita

This unisex name, although it is more common for girls, is of Ancient Greek origin and means 'unconquered'. It can also be a pet form for *Nicole* and *Nicola*.

Nina

The girl's name Nina is of Spanish and Hebrew origin and means 'little girl' or 'God is gracious'. Other sources suggest it may also mean 'mighty' and 'friendly'.

Variant forms include: *Neena, Nena, Neneh, Ninete* and *Nyna*.

Noah

The boy's name Noah is of Hebrew origin and means 'rest, comfort, long lived and peaceful'. In the Bible Noah is the patriarch who is commanded by God to build the arc and save Man and animals from extinction during the great flood.

Noel

The boy's name Noel is of French, Hebrew and Latin origin and means 'born on Christmas'. The name was traditionally given to babies born during the Christmas season.

Nora

This girl's name is of English origin and means 'woman of honour' and 'light'. It is also the feminine form of *Norman*. Despite its origin, the name is often associated with Ireland.

Variant forms include: *Noory, Norah* and *Norma*.

Norma

This uncommon girl's name is of Latin origin and means 'the norm, pattern or standard'. It could be from the Latin 'norma' (rule) in reference to a carpenter's measurement method.

Norman

The boy's name Norman is of German origin and means 'northman' or 'Norseman, conqueror', in reference to the eleventh-century Vikings. A notable bearer of the name was the British film comedian Norman Wisdom (1915-2010).

Variant forms include: *Norm, Normen* and *Normie*.

Top Ten Names Beginning with N

GIRLS	BOYS
NIAMH	NOAH
NICOLE	NATHAN
NIA	NEIL
NATALIE	NATHANIEL
NATASHA	NORMAN

Odelia

This girl's name is of German origin and means 'fortune'. It may also mean 'praise God'. It was borne by St Odilia, an eighth-century nun who founded a Benedictine convent in Alsace, France.

Odell

This girl's name is a variant of the Greek girl's name *Odele*, which means 'song'. It may also be from an Old German word, meaning 'wealth' or 'fortune'.

Variant forms include: *Odelia* and *Odile*.

Odette

The girl's name Odette is of German and French origin and means 'wealth'. In Tchaikovsky's ballet *Swan Lake* (composed 1875-76), Odette is the good swan, whereas *Odile* is the evil one.

Odile

This unisex name is of Old German origin and means 'fortunate or prosperous in battle'. In Tchaikovsky's ballet *Swan Lake* (composed 1875-76), Odile is the evil, seductive swan and *Odette* is the good swan.

Olga

This girl's name is of Old Norse and Scandinavian origin and means 'blessed, holy and successful'. Olga was a popular name in the Russian Imperial family.

Variant forms include: *Elga, Helga, Ola* and *Olia*.

Olive

The girl's name Olive is a variant of the Latin girl's name *Olivia*, and means 'olive tree'. It may also refer to the fruit and to the shade of green known as olive.

Top Ten Names in Wales

GIRLS	BOYS
RUBY	JACK
MEGAN	DYLAN
GRACE	THOMAS
CHLOE	JOSHUA
EMILY	RHYS

Oliver

This widely used and popular boy's name is of Latin origin and means 'olive tree'. It is often shortened to the pet form *Ollie*, which has become an independent name.

Variant forms include: *Olivier, Olley, Olliver* and *Ollivor*.

Olivia

The girl's name *Olivia* is of Latin origin and means 'olive tree'. It may also be the feminine form of *Oliver*. It is often shortened to the pet form *Liv*, which is an independent name of Old Norse origin, which means 'defence'.

Variant forms include: *Liv, Oliva, Olive, Olivya, Ollie* and *Olva*.

Olympia

The unusual girl's name Olympia is of Ancient Greek origin and means 'from Olympus'. Mount Olympus in Greek mythology was home to the temperamental and all-powerful Greek gods.

Omar

This boy's name is of Hebrew and Arabic origin and means 'flourishing and populous and prosperous'. Since the 1940s the name has been rising in popularity.

Variant forms include: *Omarr* and *Omer*.

Opal

The girl's name Opal or *Opall* is of Hindi and Sanskrit origin and it derives from the opal, a white gemstone. It is the birthstone for October so the name is sometimes given to babies born during that month.

Ophelia

This girl's name is of Ancient Greek origin and means 'help or profit'. It is the name of the beautiful but ill-fated maiden in Shakespeare's *Hamlet* (written between 1599 and 1601).

Oprah

This uncommon name is of Hebrew origin and means 'young deer or fawn'. African-American talk-show host Oprah Winfrey (b.1954) is a well-known bearer of the name.

Orlando

The boy's name Orlando is of Spanish origin and a variant of the Old German *Roland*, which means 'renowned land' or 'famous landowner'. In Shakespeare's comedy *As You Like It* (c.1599) the name of the hero is Orlando. A city in Florida also bears this name.

Orville

This rare boy's name is of Old French origin and means 'golden town'. This name was used by the English writer Frances Burney for a character in her eighteenth-century novel, *Evelina* (1778).

Oscar

This boy's name is of Old English origin and means 'spear of the gods', or 'gentle friend'. Often shortened to the variant pet forms, *Ossie* and *Ozzy*, which have both become independent names.

Oswald

This uncommon boy's name is of Old German origin and means 'God's power', or 'divine power', or 'rule of God'. *Osvalda* is the rare female form of Oswald.

Variant forms include: *Ossie, Osvaldo, Oswaldo, Ozzie, Ozzy* and *Waldo.*

Owen

This boy's name is of Welsh, Scottish and Greek origin and means 'born of the yew' or 'youth'. American actor and comedian Owen Wilson (b.1968) is a well-known bearer of the name.

Variant forms include: *Ewan, Ewen, Owain, Owin* and *Owynn.*

Top Ten Names Beginning with O

GIRLS	BOYS
OLIVIA	OLIVER
OPHELIA	OSCAR
ODETTE	OWEN
OLIVE	OLLIE
OPAL	OMAR

Paige

This unisex name, although it tends to be more popular for girls, is of English origin and means 'young helper or servant'. In the Middle Ages pages were well-born male servants to lords.

Variant forms include: *Page* and *Payge*.

Pamela

This widely used girl's name is of Ancient Greek origin and means 'honey or all sweetness'. It is often shortened to *Pam*, which has become an independent name.

Variant forms include: *Pamilla, Pammela, Pammie* and *Pammy*.

Paris

This unisex name is of Greek origin and it refers to the capital of France. A well-known person named Paris is American socialite Paris Hilton (b.1981).

Variant forms include: *Paras, Pares, Parris* and *Parrish*.

Patricia

This widely used girl's name is of Latin origin and means 'noble patrician'. In Roman times patricians were the highly ranked aristocratic classes. It is often shortened to the pet form *Pat*, which like another popular variant form *Patsy*, has become an independent name.

Variant forms include: *Patrica, Patrice, Patte, Pattee, Pattey, Patti, Pattie, Patty, Tricia, Trish* and *Trisha*.

Patrick

This popular boy's name is of Latin origin and means 'nobleman'. The name has Irish associations because of the fifth-century saint, Patrick, patron saint of Ireland, but its use is widespread outside Ireland.

Variant forms include: *Paddie, Paddy, Pat, Patric, Patrice* and *Patrik*.

Paul

This popular boy's name is of Latin origin and means 'small, little and humble'. In the Bible, the letters of Saint Paul, to the early Christians in the first century, form several books of the New Testament.

Variant forms include: *Pablo, Pal, Paolo, Paulo, Pavlo* and *Poul.*

Paula

The girl's name Paula is of Latin origin and means 'little and humble'. It is the feminine form of *Paul.* It was the name of several early Christian saints.

Variant forms include: *Paola, Pauletta, Paulette, Pauli, Pauline, Pollie* and *Polly.*

Paulette

The girl's name Paulette is a variant of the Latin name *Paula*, which is the feminine form of *Paul* and means 'small, little and humble'. The name is infrequently used today.

Pauline

The girl's name Pauline is a variant of the Latin name *Paula*, which has become an independent name, and means 'small, little and humble'. The name is infrequently used today.

Pearl

This girl's name is of Latin origin and means 'pearl', the jewel. The Greek form of the name is *Margaret*. It was coined in the nineteenth century when there was a vogue for jewel names.

Variant forms include: *Pearle, Pearlie, Perl, Perla, Perley, Perline, Perlita* and *Perlline.*

Peggy

This girl's name is of Greek origin and a nickname for *Margaret*, which became an independent name in the eighteenth century. It means 'pearl' and is often shortened to the nickname *Peg*.

Variant forms include: *Pegg* and *Peggie.*

Penelope/Penny

This girl's name is of Greek origin and means 'thread, web and weaver'. In Greek mythology, the name was borne by the faithful wife of Odysseus. It is often shortened to the popular nickname *Penny*, which became an independent name during the twentieth century.

Variant forms include: *Pen, Penney* and *Pennie.*

Percy

This uncommon boy's name is of Latin origin and it refers to 'one who is a skilled hunter'. It is also a shortened form of the even more uncommon name *Percival*.

Variant forms include: *Pearcy, Percey* and *Percie.*

Perdita

The girl's name Perdita is of Latin origin and means 'lost'. Shakespeare coined this uncommon name for a young heroine in his play *The Winter's Tale* (written in 1610 or 1611).

Perpetua

This girl's name is of Latin origin and means 'forever, everlasting and perpetual'. The name was borne by Saint Perpetua in the second century and has mainly been used by Roman Catholics.

Perry

This boy's name is of Latin origin and means 'traveller, stranger and wanderer'. It may also be derived from an Old English word for a person who worked or lived near pear trees.

Parrie is a variant form.

Top Ten Names in Australia

GIRLS	BOYS
ISABELLA	JACK
OLIVIA	LACHLAN
LILY	COOPER
CHLOE	WILLIAM
EMILY	JOSHUA

Peter

This classic favourite boy's name is of Greek origin and means 'stone or rock'. In the New Testament, Peter is the impulsive apostle of whom Jesus said, 'Upon this rock, I will build my faith (meaning Church)'. It is often shortened to the nickname *Pete*, which is an independent name.

Variant forms include: *Pedro, Peterson, Pierce* and *Pierre*.

Petra

The girl's name Petra is of Latin origin and means 'rock or stone'. It is the modern feminine form of *Peter*, and was adopted by English speakers in the mid-twentieth century.

Variant forms include: *Pet, Peta, Petronela, Petronella, Petronia* and *Petula*.

Petula

This girl's name is of Latin origin and means 'pertness'. It first came to prominence in the twentieth century with the British singer Petula Clark (b.1932). It may also be derived from the term 'pet'.

Philip

This boy's name is of Ancient Greek origin and means 'lover or friend of horses'. In the New Testament, Philip is one of the twelve apostles. It is often shortened to the nickname *Phil*.

Variant forms include: *Philipp, Philippe, Philippos* and *Phillip*.

Philipa

The girl's name Philipa is the feminine form of the Ancient Greek name *Philip*, which means 'friend or lover of horses'. It is sometimes shortened to the nickname *Pip*.

Variant forms include: *Phillipa, Pippa, Pippie* and *Pippy*.

Philomena

The girl's name Philomena, or *Filomena*, is of Greek origin and means 'powerful love or strongly beloved'. It was borne by the Greek princess and martyr Saint Philomena (291-304).

Phoebe

This girl's name is of Greek origin and means 'bright, pure and radiant'. It may also mean 'sweetly spoken or well spoken'. In Greek mythology it refers to Phoebus Apollo, god of light.

Variant forms include: *Febe, Pheabe, Phebe, Pheby, Phoebey* and *Phoeboe*.

Phoenix

This unisex name is of Greek origin and means 'dark red'. The beautiful phoenix bird in Arabian myth is a symbol of immortality, as it is reborn from the ashes after being consumed by flames.

Variant forms: *Fenix* and *Phenix*.

Phyllis

This girl's name is of Greek origin and means 'greenery'. In Greek mythology Phyllis is a beautiful young woman who dies for love and is transformed into an almond tree.

Variant forms include: *Filis, Fillis, Fillys, Fyllis, Philis, Phillis, Philys, Phylis* and *Phyliss*.

Pierce

This boy's name is of English origin and it is a variant of *Peter*, which means 'rock or stone'. Irish actor Pierce Brosnan (b.1953) is a well-known bearer of the name.

Variant forms include: *Pearce, Pears, Pearson, Pearsson, Peerce, Peirce* and *Piers*.

Piers

This boy's name is a popular English variant of Peter, which means 'rock or stone'. It is well known from William Langland's allegorical narrative poem *Piers Plowman* (*c*.1360–87).

Variant forms include: *Pearce, Pears, Pearson, Pierce, Pierson* and *Piersson*.

Pippa

The girl's name Pippa is a variant of *Philipa*, which means 'friend or lover of horses'. It is often shortened to the nickname *Pip*, which has become an independent name.

Polly

This girl's name is of Irish and English origin and a variant of *Molly*, which in turn is a variant of *Mary*, meaning 'star of the sea'. The name is well known from the nursery rhyme 'Polly Put the Kettle On', which was apparently adapted from an 1803 song 'Molly Put the Kettle On'. Polly is often shortened to the pet form *Poll*.

Variant forms include: *Polley, Polli, Pollie* and *Pollyanna*.

Poppy

This girl's name is of Latin origin and it refers to the flower named 'poppy'. It was first used in the late-nineteenth century when there was a vogue for flower names.

Variant forms include: *Poppi* and *Poppie*.

Preston

This boy's name is of Old English origin and means 'priest's town'. It was first used as a given name in the nineteenth century and is currently growing in popularity.

Variant forms include: *Pres, Prestan, Presten* and *Prestin*.

Primrose

This uncommon girl's name is of Latin and English origin and means 'first rose'. It is also the name for a flower (not a rose) that blooms in early spring.

Prince

This boy's name is of Latin origin and means 'prince'. The name may have originated as a nickname for someone with a lordly manner or someone who worked in a royal household.

Princess

This girl's name is of English origin and means 'princess'. Like the boy's name *Prince*, it may have originated as a nickname for someone with a ladylike manner.

Priscilla

This girl's name is of Latin origin and means 'venerable, old and ancient'. It is sometimes shortened to the pet name *Cilla*, which has become an independent name.

Variant forms include: *Priscella, Priscila, Priscylla, Prisila, Prisilla, Prissy* and *Prysilla*.

Prudence

This girl's name is of Latin and English origin and means 'caution, prudence and discretion'. A virtue name, it was popular in the seventeenth and nineteenth centuries, but is less common today.

Variant forms include: *Pru, Prudie, Prudy* and *Prue.*

Prunella

This girl's name is of Latin origin and means 'tiny plum'. The British actress Prunella Scales (b.1932), famous for her role in the classic TV comedy *Fawlty Towers*, is a well-known bearer of this name.

Top Ten Names Beginning with P

GIRLS	BOYS
POPPY	PETER
PHOEBE	PAUL
PAIGE	PRESTON
PIPPA	PRINCE
PRISCILLA	PIERS

Quade

This boy's name is of Gaelic origin. It is derived from McQuade, a Scottish clan name. It may also be of German origin and mean 'son of Walter', or 'cross-tempered one'.

Variant forms include: *Quaid* and *Quaide*.

Queenie

This uncommon girl's name is of English origin and it simply means 'queen' or 'royal monarch'. It may have originated as a nickname for someone with regal airs.

Quentin

This boy's name is of Latin origin and means 'fifth' or 'fifth-born son' or 'born in the fifth month – May'. British author Quentin Crisp (1908–99) and American filmmaker Quentin Tarantino (b.1963) are controversial and well-known bearers of the name.

Variant forms include: *Quent, Quenten, Quenton, Quint, Quinten, Quintin* and *Quinton*.

Quincy

This boy's name is of French origin and means 'estate of the fifth son' and 'to counsel'. Used largely by English speakers, Quincy is an uncommon name.

Variant forms include: *Quin, Quincey, Quinn,* and *Quinsy*.

Quinlan

The unusual boy's name Quinlan, and its variant spelling *Quinlen*, is of Irish and Gaelic origin and means 'one who is fit and strong' or 'descendent of the slender one'.

Quinn

This boy's name is of Irish and Gaelic origin and means 'to counsel'. Quinn is also an English shortened form of *Quentin* and *Quincy*.

Variant forms include: *Quin, Quinlan* and *Quinnell.*

Top Ten Names Associated with Genius

GIRLS	BOYS
MARIE	ALBERT
ROSALIND	STEPHEN
SOPHIE	ALFRED
CAROLINE	THOMAS
MARGARET	ALEXANDER

Rachel

This popular girl's name is of Hebrew origin and means 'ewe'. In the Old Testament, Jacob's wife, Rachel, is described as being 'beautiful in form'.

Variant forms include: *Rachael, Racheal, Rachele, Racheli, Rachell, Rachelle, Rae, Raechel, Raechell, Raquel, Raquela, Raquella, Raquelle, Raychel, Raychelle, Raye* and *Rechell*.

Rae

This girl's name is a shortened version of *Rachel* and the feminine form of *Ray*. It is sometimes used as a boy's name, but is more popular for girls.

Variant forms include: *Raeann, Raeanna, Raeanne, Raelene, Raylene, Raylina, Rayma, Rayna, Raynelle* and *Rayona*.

Raina

This girl's name is of Latin origin and means 'queen'. It is the feminine form of *Ray* and the name first appeared for the heroine Raina in the play *Arms and the Man* (1894) by George Bernard Shaw.

Variant forms include: *Raene, Raine, Rainee, Rainelle, Rainey, Raya, Raylene, Raylina, Rayline, Reina, Reyna* and *Reyney*.

Ralph

This boy's name is of Old English origin and means 'wise and strong wolf' and 'counsel'. *Rolf* is the German variant form of the name. It is also a variant of *Rudolph*.

Variant forms include: *Rafe, Raff, Raoul, Raul* and *Rolph*.

Ramona

This girl's name is of Spanish and German origin and means 'well-advised protector'. The name was popularised in the late-nineteenth century with the American novel *Ramona* (1884) by Helen Hunt Jackson.

Variant forms include: *Rae, Ramee, Ramie, Ramonda, Ramonde, Ramonna, Remona, Remonna, Romona, Romonda* and *Romonia*.

Ramsay

The unusual boy's name Ramsay is of Old English origin and means 'from the raven's or ram's island'. It is mainly used in the Gaelic and English languages.

Variant forms include: *Ramsy, Ramsey, Ramzey* and *Ramzi*.

Randolph

This boy's name is of Old German origin and means 'wolf shield' and 'strong defender'. It is often shortened to the pet form *Randy*, which has become an independent name for both boys and girls. In English slang, randy means 'amorous'. *Randal* is a boy's only variant.

Variant forms include: *Randie, Randall, Randell, Randolf* and *Ranulph*.

Raphael

This boy's name is of Hebrew origin and means 'God has healed'. Raphael does not appear in the Bible, but is one of the seven archangels in the apocryphal *Book of Tobias*, which is believed to have been written in the second century BC.

Variant forms include: *Rafal, Rafael, Rafaelle, Rafello, Raffael, Raffaello, Raphaello, Raphello* and *Ravel*.

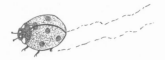

Raquel

This girl's name is a Spanish and Portuguese variant of the popular girl's name *Rachel*, which means 'female sheep'. American actress Raquel Welch (b.1940) is a famous bearer of the name.

Variant forms include: *Racquel, Raquela, Raquelle* and *Roquel.*

Ray

This unisex name, although it tends to be used more for boys, is of English origin and a shortened version of *Raymond*, which has become an independent name.

Variant forms include: *Rae, Rai, Raye* and *Reigh.*

Raymond

This boy's name is of Old German origin, and means 'well-advised protector'. Raymond Blanc (b.1949), the award-winning chef, is a well-known bearer of the name. The name, which was popular in the 1950s, is often shortened to *Ray.*

Variant forms include: *Raimond, Raymund, Raynor, Reymond* and *Reymundo.*

Reanna

This girl's name is of Celtic origin and is a variant of the Welsh name *Rhiannon*, which means 'nymph' or 'goddess'. Some sources suggest it may also mean 'to flow, and river, stream'.

Variant forms include: *Reannah, Reanne, Reannon* and *Reeanne.*

Rebecca

The widely used girl's name Rebecca is of Hebrew origin and means 'to bind', in reference to the bonds of marriage. It could also mean 'cattle stall'. The name was popularised by Daphne du Maurier's novel *Rebecca* (1938).

Variant forms include: *Becca, Beck, Becka, Becke, Beckee, Becky, Rebbecca, Rebeca, Rebeccah* and *Rebeccea.*

Red

The boy's name Red, or *Redd*, is of English origin and it refers to the colour red. It may have originated as a nickname for someone with a ruddy complexion or red hair.

Top Ten
Celebrity Baby Names

The most-copied names.

GIRLS	BOYS
LOLA	LENNON
LEXI	BROOKLYN
LIBERTY	DEVON
SURI	CRUZ
SHILOH	ROMEO

Reese

This unisex name is of Welsh origin and means 'enthusiasm and ardour'. Oscar-winning, American actress Reese Witherspoon (b.1976) is a well-known bearer of the name.

Reece is a variant form.

Regina

This girl's name is of Latin origin and means 'queen'. The name became popular at the end of the Victorian era because Queen Victoria was known as Victoria Regina. It also refers to the Virgin Mary.

Variant forms include: *Reginia, Reina, Reyna* and *Rina*.

Reginald

This boy's name is of Latin and German origin and means 'well-advised ruler' or 'advisor to the ruler'. It is often shortened to *Reggie*, which has become a fairly popular independent name.

Variant forms include: *Reg, Reynold, Reynolds, Rinaldo* and *Ronald*.

Renata

The girl's name Renata is of Latin origin and means 'reborn' or 'born again'. It is a variant of *Renée*, and is predominately used in the Italian, Spanish and German languages.

Variant forms include: *Rene, Rennay* and *Rennie.*

Rene

The unisex name Rene is a shortened form of *Irene*, which means 'peaceful', and since the beginning of the twentieth century it has become an independent name.

Variant forms include: *Reney, Renie* and *Rennie.*

Renée

This girl's name is of French origin and means 'rebirth'. It is a variant of *Renata*. Oscar-winning, American actress Renée Zellweger (b.1969) is a famous bearer of the name.

Reuben

The uncommon boy's name Reuben is of Hebrew origin and means 'behold, or see a son'. In the Old Testament, Reuben is the first-born of Jacob's twelve sons.

Variant forms include: *Reuban, Reubin, Ruben* and *Rubin.*

Rex

The boy's name Rex is of Latin origin and means 'the king'. Oscar-winning, British actor Rex Harrison (1908–90) was a well-known bearer of the name.

Rhett

This boy's name is of Latin origin and means 'speaker'. The name is familiar as the hero of Margaret Mitchell's romantic novel *Gone With The Wind* (1936), which was made into a film (1939) starring Clark Gable as Rhett.

Rhiannon

This girl's name is of Welsh origin and means 'nymph, goddess and great queen'. First used as a given name in the twentieth century, in Welsh mythology the name was borne by the horse goddess.

Variant forms include: *Reanna, Rheanna, Rheanne, Rhiana, Rhiann, Rhianna, Rhiannan, Rhianon, Riana* and *Rianon*.

Rhoda

This girl's name is of Ancient Greek origin and means 'rose' and 'woman from Rhodes'. The name's popularity was given a small boost from the American TV sitcom *Rhoda* (1974-78).

Variant forms include: *Rhodie, Roda, Rodi, Rodie* and *Rodina*.

Rhona

This girl's name is the feminine form of *Ronald*. It may also be derived from the place name of the Hebridean island, Rona ('rough isle') on which Saint Rona lived.

Roana is a variant form.

Rhonda

This unusual girl's name is of Welsh origin and means 'good spear'. It may also be derived from the river valley in Wales, which is named after the River Rhondda, meaning 'speaking aloud'.

Variant forms include: *Rhonnda, Ronda, Rondi* and *Ronnda*.

Rhys

This boy's name is of Welsh origin and it is literally derived from the word 'rhys', which means 'enthusiasm', 'ardour' and 'rashness'. It is also a variant of *Reese*.

Richard

This enduringly popular boy's name is of Old German origin from 'ric' meaning 'power' and 'hard' meaning 'strong', interpreted as 'powerful leader'. The name was introduced to England by the Normans, and is often shortened to the nickname *Dick*. Prominent bearers of the name include kings of England, and the US President Richard Nixon (1913-94).

Variant forms include: *Rich, Rick, Ricky* and *Rico*.

Riley

This unisex name, although it is more common for boys, is of Old English origin from 'ryge' meaning 'rye' and 'leah' meaning 'clearing'. The name's popularity has been rising steadily since the 1960s.

Rina

This girl's name is an eclectic mix of the Greek names *Irene* and *Katherine*, the Latin name *Regina*, the Hebrew name *Rena*, and other names ending with 'rina'. It means 'peace', 'reborn', 'queen', 'joyful' and 'clear'.

Rita

This girl's name is an abbreviated form of the Spanish name *Margarita* (*Margaret*) meaning 'pearl'. A famous bearer of the name was Rita Hayworth (Margarita Carmen Cansino, 1918-87).

Top Ten Famous Chef Names

GIRLS	BOYS
DELIA	GORDON
NIGELLA	JAMIE
JULIA	RAYMOND
RACHAEL	ANTHONY
PAULA	MARCO

Robert

This boy's name is of Old German origin, from 'hrod' meaning 'fame' and 'behrt' meaning 'bright', interpreted as meaning 'famously famous'. Robert the Bruce (1274-1329) was the king of the Scots who secured Scotland's independence from England. Robert is consistently among the most popular names in the English-speaking world.

Variant forms include: *Bert, Bob, Bobbie, Bobby, Rob* and *Robbie.*

Roberta

This girl's name is of Old English and Old German origin and means 'bright flame' or 'famous one' or 'famously bright'. It is the feminine form of *Robert.*

Variant forms include: *Berta, Bertie, Berty, Robby, Robena, Robenia, Roberda, Robernetta, Robertena, Robertina, Robi* and *Robin.*

Robin

This unisex name is of English origin and is a variant of *Robert.* It has been in popular use as a boy's name since the Middle Ages and the legend of Robin Hood. For girls there is the association with the robin, red-breasted songbird.

Variant forms include: *Robbin, Robbyn* and *Robyn.*

Robson

This boy's name is a variant of *Robert,* which means 'bright flame' and 'famously bright'. It could also be a variant of *Robinson,* which means 'son of Robert'.

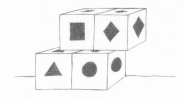

190

Rocco

This boy's name is of German and Italian origin and means 'to rest or repose'. It may also mean 'battle cry'. *Rocky* is a common nickname for Rocco and its variant form *Rocko.*

Rochelle

This girl's name is of German and Italian origin and means 'to rest'. It may also mean 'to roar' and is the feminine form of *Rocco*. It is often shortened to the nickname *Shell.*

Variant forms include: *Roch, Rochele, Rochell* and *Roshelle.*

Rocky

Rocky is a common nickname for *Rocco* (and its variant form *Rocko*). It has become an independent name associated with physical toughness because of the famous American boxer Rocky Marciano (1923-69).

Rod

The boy's name Rod, and its variant form *Rodd*, is a shortened version of *Roderick*, meaning 'famous power', and *Rodney*, meaning 'fame' or 'island'. It has become an independent name.

Roderick

This widely used boy's name is of Old German and English origin and means 'famous power' or 'famously powerful'. It is often shortened to the nickname *Rod.*

Variant forms include: *Rhoderick, Rhodric, Rodd, Rodderick, Roddie, Roddric, Roddrick, Roddy, Roderic, Rodric, Rodrick, Rodrigo* and *Rodrik.*

Rodney

This boy's name is of Old English origin and means 'fame' and 'island near the clearing'. Originally a surname, it began to appear as a popular first name in the early nineteenth century.

Roger

This boy's name is of Old German origin and means 'famous warrior or spearman'. The name was popular in the Middle Ages and was revived in the nineteenth and twentieth centuries.

Variant forms include: *Rodge, Rodger* and *Rogers.*

Roland

This boy's name is of Old German origin and means 'renowned landowner'. The name was borne by the heroic knight of the court of Charlemagne, whose story can be found in the twelfth-century *The Song of Roland*.

Variant forms include: *Rolando, Rolland* and *Rowland*.

Rolf

This boy's name is a variant of the Old German name 'Rudolph', which means 'wise and strong' and 'famous wolf'. It is also a variant of the boy's name *Ralph*.

Variant forms include: *Rolfe, Rolph* and *Rowland*.

Roman

This boy's name is of Latin origin and means 'man of Rome'. In ancient times being a citizen of Rome was a badge of honour and courage. It is sometimes shortened to the nickname *Rome*.

Romeo

This boy's name is of Latin origin and means 'citizen of Rome, or pilgrim to Rome'. It has been immortalised by the tragic hero in Shakespeare's play *Romeo and Juliet* (written between 1591 and 1596).

Ronald

This boy's name is of Old Norse origin and means 'well-advised ruler'. It is often shortened to the nickname *Ron*. American President Ronald Reagan (1911–2004) was a famous bearer of the name.

Variant forms include: *Ronaldo, Ronn, Ronnie* and *Ronny*.

Ronan

This boy's name is of Irish and Gaelic origin and means 'little seal'. The name was borne by a fifth or sixth-century Irish saint who was a missionary in Cornwall and Brittany.

Variant forms include: *Ronen, Ronin* and *Ronnan*.

Rory

This unisex name, although it tends to be more popular for boys, is of Irish and Gaelic origin and means 'red king'. Some sources suggest it may also mean 'famously bright' and 'royal poet'.

Variant forms include: *Rorey* and *Rorry*.

Rosa

This girl's name is the Latinate version of the name *Rose*, which means 'rose' and was first used in the nineteenth century. In Bulgarian the meaning is 'dew'.

Rosalie

This girl's name is of French origin and a variant of the Italian *Rosalia*, which means 'rose' or possibly 'rose garden'. It is also a variant of *Rose*.

Variant forms include: *Rosa, Rosalee, Rosalina, Rosalind* and *Rosaline*.

Rosalind

This girl's name is of Old German origin and means 'gentle horse'. Often shortened to the nickname *Ros*. It is also a poetic creation by the sixteenth-century poet, Edmund Spenser, with the meaning 'pretty rose'.

Variant forms include: *Rosalen, Rosalina, Roselin, Roselina, Roselyn, Rosina, Roslyn* and *Roz*.

Rosalyn

The girl's name Rosalyn is a fairly recent, and popular, variant of *Rosalind* and also a combination of the names *Rose* and *Lynn*, with the meaning 'pretty rose'.

Variant forms include: *Rosalin, Rosalynn, Roselynn, Roslyn* and *Rozlynn*.

Rosamund

The fairly uncommon girl's name Rosamund is of Old German origin and means 'horse protector'. Other sources suggest that it also means 'pure rose' and 'rose of the world'.

Rosanna

This girl's name is a popular variant of the English name *Roseanne*, which was first used in the eighteenth century as a combination of the names *Rose* and *Anne*.

Rose

This girl's name is of Latin origin and means 'rose', the flower often associated with the Virgin Mary. Some sources suggest that it also means 'horse' and 'fame'.

Variant forms include: *Rosa, Rosaleen, Rosalia, Rosalie, Rosalin, Rosalind, Rosaline, Rosalinn, Rosalynn, Rosie* and *Rosy*.

Rosemary

The girl's name Rosemary is of Latin and English origin and means 'sea dew'. It may also refer to the fragrant herb, and be a combination of *Mary* and *Rose*.

Top Ten Nature Names

GIRLS	BOYS
DAWN	ASH
PEARL	RIVER
APPLE	LEE
FERN	ROCKY
ROSE	CLAY

Rosie

The girl's name Rosie, and its variant spelling *Rosy*, is a popular variant of the classic names *Rose* and *Rosemary.* The rose flower is a symbol of many things, including love, the Virgin Mary and England, ensuring its popularity as a classic favourite girl's name.

Ross

This boy's name has its origins in the Celtic language and means 'red', 'famous', 'horse' and 'peninsula'. The name became well known from a character in the American TV sitcom *Friends* (1994–2004).

Rowan

This boy's name is from the Gaelic 'Ruadhan' meaning 'little red-headed one'. The name was borne by two Irish saints in the fifth and sixth centuries.

Rowena

This girl's name is of Old English origin and means, 'fame', 'happiness', 'slender', 'blessed' and 'holy'. The name was borne by a legendary daughter of Hengest, the fifth-century Anglo-Saxon leader.

Variant forms include: *Rhowena, Roweena, Rowenna* and *Rowina.*

Roxanne

This girl's name is of Persian origin and means 'dawn'. It is often shortened to the nicknames *Roxi, Roxie* or *Roxy.* It was made famous by the 1978 hit song 'Roxanne', by the rock band The Police.

Variant forms include: *Roxane, Roxann, Roxanna, Roxine* and *Roxyanna.*

Roy

This boy's name is of Irish and Gaelic origin and means 'red or ruddy-haired one'. It could also be a shortened form of *Royston* or the French name *Leroy*, which means 'king'.

Royston

This boy's name is of Old English origin and means 'settlement of Royce' or 'son of Roy'. It is often shortened to the nickname *Roy*, which has become an independent name.

Variant forms include: *Roiston* and *Royce*.

Ruby

Ruby is of English origin and refers to the precious 'red gemstone'. It was a widely used name in the early twentieth century, then its usage dropped, but now it is very popular again.

Variant forms include: *Rubee, Rubena, Rubey, Rubi* and *Rubie*.

Rudolph

This boy's name is of Old German origin and means 'famous or renowned wolf'. The well-known Christmas song, 'Rudolph the Red-Nosed Reindeer' (1964), has not increased the name's popularity.

Variant forms include: *Rolf, Rolph, Rudi, Rudie, Rudolf, Rudolfo* and *Rudy*.

Rufus

This boy's name is of Latin origin and means 'red-haired one'. Originally a Roman nickname, it was first used by English speakers in the nineteenth century.

Rupert

This boy's name is of German origin and means 'famously bright'. It is a variant of *Robert*. The British actor Rupert Grint (b.1988), of *Harry Potter* movie fame, is a well-known bearer of the name.

Russ

The boy's name Russ is a shortened form of the Old French name *Russell* or its variant form *Russel,* which means 'little red'. It has become an independent name.

Russel / Russell

This boy's name is of Old French origin and means 'little red', probably originating as a nickname for someone with red hair or a ruddy complexion. Australian actor Russell Crowe (b.1964) is a well-known bearer of the name.

Ruth

This girl's name is a Hebrew name of uncertain derivation, but often interpreted as meaning 'friend, companion' and 'vision of beauty'. The story of devoted Ruth, with her famous words 'Wherever you go, I go...', is told in the Bible in the book of Ruth and, as a result, the name has traditionally been associated with sympathy and compassion.

Ruthie is a variant form.

Ryan

This boy's name is of Gaelic origin and means 'king'. It may also mean 'descendent of Rian'. It is currently a popular name borne by the Canadian actor Ryan Reynolds (b.1976).

Variant forms include: *Rian, Rion, Ryann, Ryen, Ryon* and *Ryun.*

Top Ten Names Beginning with R

GIRLS	BOYS
RUBY	RYAN
REBECCA	RILEY
ROSIE	RHYS
ROSE	REECE
RUTH	ROBERT

Sabrina

This girl's name is of Celtic origin. In Celtic mythology, Sabrina is the name of a goddess maiden who gives her name to the River Severn. It is often shortened to the nickname *Bree*.

Variant forms include: *Sabreen, Sabreena, Sabrena, Sabrene, Sabrinna, Sabryna, Sebreena, Sebrina* and *Zabrina*.

Sade

The girl's name Sade is of African origin and means 'princess' and 'honour bestows the crown'. Nigerian singer Sade Abu (b.1959) influenced the popularity of the name.

Sadie

This girl's name is a variant form of the Hebrew name *Sarah*, which means 'princess'. It became an independent name in the nineteenth century. In Latin, Sadie may also mean 'mercy and grace'.

Variant forms include: *Sada, Sadah, Sade, Saidee, Saidey, Saidie* and *Saydie*.

Sally

This girl's name is of English origin and a variant of the Hebrew name *Sarah*, which means 'princess', and 'lady'. It is often shortened to the nickname *Sal*.

Variant forms include: *Sallee, Salley, Sallianne, Sallie* and *Sallyann*.

Salome

This girl's name is of Hebrew origin and means 'peace'. In the New Testament, Salome is the beautiful and seductive woman who dances for King *Herod* and demands the head of John the Baptist on a platter as her reward.

Variant forms include: *Salma, Salmah, Saloma, Salomi, Selima, Selma* and *Solome*.

Sam

This widely used unisex name is a shortened form of *Samantha* for girls and *Samuel* for boys, which has become an independent name. The name tends to be more popular for boys.

Samantha

This girl's name is of Hebrew origin and the feminine form of *Samuel*, which means 'God heard'. It also contains a Greek word meaning 'flower' and is often shortened to the unisex nickname *Sam*. The name became popular in the 1960s due to the *Bewitched* (1964-72) TV series and again in recent years due to the *Sex And The City* TV series (1998-2004) and movies (2008, 2010).

Variant forms include: *Samey, Sami, Sammantha, Sammee, Sammey, Sammie* and *Symantha*.

Samuel

The boy's name Samuel is of Hebrew origin and means 'God heard', or 'asked of God', or 'God's heart', or 'God's name'. It is often shortened to the unisex nickname *Sam*.

Sandra

The girl's name Sandra is of Ancient Greek origin and means 'defender or protector of me'. It is a variant form of *Alexander*. Oscar-winning, American actress Sandra Bullock (b.1964) is a well-known bearer of this name.

Variant forms include: *Sanda, Sandee, Sandi, Sandie, Sandy* and *Sondra*.

Sandy

This unisex name is of Ancient Greek origin. It is a pet form of the names *Alexander* and *Sandra* that has become an independent name. It is also a nickname for someone with sandy coloured hair.

Sapphire

This girl's name is of Hebrew origin and refers to the sapphire, the precious blue gemstone that is the jewel for September. The name was first adopted, along with other birthstone names, in the nineteenth century.

Sara

The widely used girl's name Sara is a popular variant of the Hebrew name *Sarah*, which means 'princess', or 'lady'. *Sadie* and *Sally* are other widely used variant forms.

Sarah

This enduringly popular girl's name is of Hebrew origin with the meaning 'princess, lady'. In the Old Testament, Sarah is the very beautiful wife of Abraham.

Variant forms include: *Sadie, Sally, Sara, Sari, Sarra, Sarrah* and *Zara*.

Sasha

This unisex name is of Russian origin and is a variant of the Greek boy's name *Alexander*, which means 'man's defender'. The name tends to be more popular for girls.

Saskia

This girl's name is of Danish and German origin and means 'the Saxon people'. It could also mean 'valley of light'. The name could also be a variant of *Sasha*.

Scarlett

This girl's name is of Old French origin and means 'red cloth'. It became popular as a first name after Scarlett O'Hara, the heroine in Margaret Mitchell's novel *Gone With the Wind* (1936).

Variant forms include: *Scarlet* and *Scarlette*.

Scott

This boy's name is of Old English and Celtic origin and means 'Scotsman' or 'from the priest's house'. Despite its ancient origins the name was mainly used in the twentieth century.

Variant forms include: *Scot, Scottie* and *Scotty*.

Seamus

This boy's name is of Irish origin and a variant of the Hebrew name *James*, which means 'he who supplants'. The variant form *Shamus* is also American slang for a private detective.

Sean

This boy's name is of Irish origin and a variant of the Hebrew name *John*, which means 'God is merciful' or 'God is gracious'. The name only spread outside Ireland in the twentieth century.

Variant forms include: *Shane, Shaun* and *Shawn*.

Sebastian

This boy's name is of Ancient Greek origin and means 'respected and venerable'. It may also mean 'man from Sebasta', a town in Asia Minor. It is often shortened to the nickname *Seb*.

Variant forms include: *Sabastian, Seb, Sebastien* and *Sebestyen*.

Selina

This girl's name is of Ancient Greek origin and means 'moon, light, heaven and shining'. In Greek mythology the name was borne by the goddess of the moon, Selene.

Top Ten Names Considered Sexy

GIRLS	BOYS
CERISE	ADAM
CHERYL	BRAD
MARILYN	CLINT
NATALIE	DAVID
PAMELA	JUSTIN

Selwyn

This uncommon boy's name is of Old English origin and means 'manor friend'. It is also a variant of the rarely used Latin boy's name *Silvanus*, and the shortened form, *Silas*, which means 'woods'.

Serena

This girl's name is of Latin origin and means 'serene, clear and calm'. American tennis champion Serena Williams (b.1981) is a well-known bearer of the name.

Variant forms include: *Reena, Sarina, Saryna, Sereena, Serene, Serenity, Serenna, Serina, Serinah, Serinna* and *Seryna.*

Sergei

This boy's name is of Russian and English origin and means 'servant and attendant'. It is a variant of *Sergio*. The fourteenth-century Saint Sergius is a much-loved Russian saint.

Seth

This boy's name is of Hebrew origin and means 'appointed or set'. By the nineteenth century the name had acquired something of a rural flavour in the UK. In Sanskrit the name means 'bridge'.

Seymour

This boy's name is of Old French origin and means 'from Saint-Maur', the place name in Northern France. Some Norman aristocrats who conquered England in 1066 were known by the names of the places they originally came from.

Shane

This popular boy's name is a variant of the Irish *Sean*, and the Hebrew *John*, meaning 'God's grace or mercy'. The name revived after the publication of the popular Western novel *Shane* (1949) by Jack Schaefer.

Variant forms include: *Shaine, Shayn* and *Shayne.*

Shannon

This unisex name is of Celtic origin and means 'old, wise, one of the river'. It could be derived from the River Shannon, the longest river in Ireland, but might also be a variant of *Sharon*.

Variant forms include: *Shane, Shannan, Shannen* and *Shanon.*

Sharon

This widely used girl's name is of Hebrew origin and means 'singer' and 'a fertile plain'. It is also a biblical place name referring to land at the foot of Mount Carmel in Israel.

Variant forms include: *Sharan, Shareen, Sharen, Sharren, Sharrin, Sharron, Sharronne, Sharyn, Sheena, Sheran* and *Sheron.*

Sheena

This girl's name, and its variant spelling *Shena*, is an Irish variant of the widely used Hebrew name *Jane*, meaning 'God is gracious' and 'God is merciful'.

Sheila

This girl's name is of Irish and Gaelic origin and means 'blind'. 'Sheela' is a Hindu term for 'gentle', while in Australian slang a 'Shelia' means a woman. It could also be a variant of *Cilla.*

Variant forms include: *Sheilia, Shela, Shelia, Shella, Sheyla, Shiela, Shila, Shilah* and *Shilea.*

Sheldon

This boy's name, and its variant spellings *Shelden* and *Sheldan*, is of Old English origin and means 'steep valley'. This place name can be found in several parts of England, including Devon.

Shelley

This unisex name, although it is more popular for girls, is of Old English and German origin and means 'bright meadow' and 'powerful ruler'. It is often shortened to the nickname *Shell.*

Variant forms include: *Shellie* and *Shelly.*

Sheridan

This unisex name, although it tends to be slightly more popular for boys, is of Irish and Gaelic origin and means 'seeker'. It may also mean 'peaceful, wild man'.

Variant forms: *Sheredan, Sheridon* and *Sherridan*.

Sherlock

This boy's name is of English origin and means 'shear lock'. It probably derived as a nickname for someone with short hair, but is more familiar as the name of the fictional detective, Sherlock Holmes, created by Sir *Arthur* Conan Doyle (1859-1930) in the late-nineteenth century.

Shiloh

This unisex name is of Hebrew origin and means 'his gift'. Well known as the name of the first biological daughter (b.2006) of American movie stars *Angelina* Jolie (b.1975) and Brad Pitt (b.1963).

Shirley

This girl's name is of Old English origin and means 'bright meadow'. Often shortened to the nickname *Shirl*, it was popularised through the fame of the American child star Shirley Temple (b.1928).

Variant forms include: *Sherlee, Sherli, Sherlie, Shirlee, Shirly* and *Shurlee*.

Shona

The girl's name Shona is of Irish and Gaelic origin and a variant of *Sheena* and *Joan*. It is also the feminine form of *John*.

Variant forms include: *Shone* and *Shuna*.

Sian

This girl's name is of Welsh origin and a variant of the Hebrew name *Jane*, which means 'God is gracious' or 'God is merciful'. It may also be a variant of *Jean*.

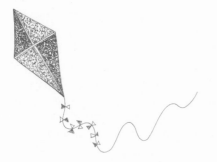

Sidney

This unisex name is of Old English origin and means 'wide meadow' or 'wide island'. First used in the eighteenth century, it became popular as a first name in the nineteenth century.

Variant forms include: *Sydney, Sideny, Sidneigh, Sidni* and *Sidnie*.

Sienna

This girl's name and its original spelling, *Siena*, is of Latin origin and means 'from Siena', an Italian city famous for its art. The name also refers to a reddish shade of brown.

Sigmund

This boy's name is of Old German origin and means 'victorious protector or defender'. The name is well known to many because of the Austrian psychoanalyst Sigmund Freud (1856-1939).

Sigourney

This girl's name was originally a surname and appeared as a first name in novelist F. Scott Fitzgerald's novel *The Great Gatsby* (1925). It was made famous by American actress Sigourney Weaver (b.1949).

Silvia

This girl's name is of Latin origin and means 'woods, forest'. Silvia was an Ancient Roman nature goddess. Shakespeare used the name for a heroine in his comedy *The Two Gentleman of Verona* (written in 1590 or 1591).

Variant forms include: *Silva, Silvana, Silvanna, Silvestra, Silvie, Sylvia* and *Sylvie*.

Simon

This enduringly popular boy's name is of Hebrew origin and means 'God has heard' or 'He hears'. The name of two disciples in the New Testament, Simon has been a popular name from the Middle Ages onwards. It is often shortened to the nickname *Si*.

Variant forms include: *Simeon, Simone, Simpson, Symms, Syms* and *Szymon*.

Simone

This girl's name is the feminine French form of the boy's name *Simon*, which means 'God hears'. From the middle of the twentieth century the name has been used outside France.

Sinclair

This boy's name is of English and French origin and means 'from Saint Clair', a place name in Northern France. It may also mean 'clear pool' or 'clear well'.

Variant forms include: *Sinclaire, Sinclare* and *Synclair*.

Sinead

This girl's name, and its variant spelling *Shinead*, is of Irish origin. It is a variant of *Jane* and *Janet*, which are feminine forms of *John*, meaning 'God's grace and mercy'.

Siobhan

This girl's name is of Irish origin and a variant of *Jane*, which is a feminine form of *John*, meaning 'God's grace or mercy'. The name is in irregular use today.

Variant forms include: *Chevonne, Chivon, Shavaun, Shavon, Shavonne, Shirvaun, Shivahn, Sioban, Siobahn, Siobhian* and *Syvonne*.

Skye

This unisex name – also spelt *Sky* – is of English origin and simply means 'sky'. The name was infrequently used before the 1980s, but has been steadily growing in popularity since then.

Solomon

This boy's name is of Hebrew origin and means 'peace'. In the Old Testament, Solomon succeeded his father David as King of Israel and was renowned for his proverbial wisdom.

Sonia

This girl's name is of English origin and a variant of *Sophia*, which means 'wisdom'. It is predominately used in the English language. *Sonya* is the Russian and Scandinavian variant.

Sophia

This popular girl's name is of Ancient Greek origin and means 'wisdom'. The twentieth-century revival of interest in the name may be due to Oscar-winning, Italian actress Sophia Loren (b.1934).

Variant forms include: *Sofia* and *Sophie*.

Top Ten Names Suggesting Femininity or Masculinity

GIRLS	BOYS
ISABELLA	LUKE
ANNA	ARTHUR
EMMA	HARLEY
ELIZABETH	HARRISON
JESSICA	GRANT

Sophie

The girl's name Sophie is a variant (probably French) of the Ancient Greek name *Sophia*, which means 'wisdom'. It is regarded as traditional and feminine and is currently a popular name.

Spencer

This occupational name, and its variant spelling *Spenser*, is of Old French and English origin and means 'steward or dispenser of provisions'. It is often shortened to the nickname *Spence.*

Spike

This boy's name is of English origin and means 'spike'. Adopted as a first name in the twentieth century, it was originally a nickname for someone whose name was unknown.

Stacey

This unisex name, although it is more popular for girls, is of English origin and a variant of the Greek name *Anastasia*, which means 'resurrection'. It is often shortened to the nickname *Stace.*

Variant forms include: *Stacy* and *Staycey.*

Stafford

This boy's name is of Old English origin and means 'ford by a landing place'. It was used regularly in the nineteenth century but is considered unusual today.

Stanley

This boy's name is of Old English origin and means 'stone meadow or clearing'. It is often shortened to the nickname *Stan*, which has become an independent name.

Variant forms include: *Stanlea, Stanlee* and *Stanly*.

Stella

This girl's name is of Latin origin and was initially from 'Stella Maris', a title for the Virgin Mary meaning 'star of the sea'. From the Middle Ages it was used to refer to the brilliance and beauty of a star.

Variant forms include: *Estella, Estelle, Stela* and *Stelle*.

Stephanie

This widely used girl's name is of Greek origin and means 'crown or garland'. It is the feminine form of *Stephen* and is often shortened to the nickname *Steph*.

Variant forms include: *Stefana, Stefani, Stefanie, Stefenney, Stepfanie, Stephanine* and *Stephany*.

Stephen

This popular boy's name is of Ancient Greek origin and means 'crowned' or 'crown or garland'. In the Bible the name was borne by the first Christian martyr. It is often shortened to the nickname *Steve*. Stefan is the German, Scandinavian and Slavic form of the name.

Variant forms include: *Stefan, Stefano, Steffan, Stephan, Stevan, Steven, Stevenson, Stevie* and *Stevy*.

Stewart

This boy's name is of Old English origin and is derived from a Scottish surname, which was in turn derived from an occupation title for a 'steward or attendant'.

Variant forms include: *Steward* and *Stuart*.

Stirling

This boy's name, and its variant spelling *Sterling*, is of English origin and means 'little star'. The name is also associated with 'excellence' and with things that are of 'high quality' and 'genuine'.

Stuart

This boy's name is a popular variant of the Old English name *Stewart*, which means 'steward or attendant'. It is often shortened to the nickname *Stu* or *Stew*.

Sue

This girl's name is a shortened version of the Hebrew name *Susan*, which means 'lily'. It has become an independent name, and it may also be a shortened form of *Susannah*.

Sukey

This girl's name is a shortened form of the Hebrew *Susan*, which means 'lily'. The name was first used in the eighteenth century, fell out of popularity and was revived again in the twentieth century.

Sukie is a variant form.

Summer

This girl's name is of Old English origin and refers to the season of summer. The name has grown in popularity since the 1960s, before that it was only modestly used.

Variant forms: *Somer, Sommers* and *Summers*.

Suri

This girl's name is of Hebrew origin and means 'princess'. It may also mean 'knife' or 'red rose'. The name has grown in popularity since American movie stars Tom Cruise (b.1962) and Katie Holmes (b.1978) named their daughter Suri (b.2006).

Susan

This widely used girl's name is of Hebrew origin and means 'lily'. It is also a shortened form of *Susannah*, and is often shortened to the nicknames *Sue* or *Susie*.

Variant forms include: *Sukie, Susana, Susann, Susanna, Suzan* and *Suzana*.

Susanna

This girl's name is the original form of the Hebrew name *Susan*, which means 'lily'. It was first adopted by English speakers in the Middle Ages and remains widely used to this day.

Variant forms include: *Susana, Suzanne* and *Suzannah*.

Sylvester

This boy's name is of Latin origin and means 'wooded'. It is often shortened to the nickname *Sly*. American actor Sylvester Stallone (b.1946) is a famous bearer of the name.

Variant forms include: *Silvester* and *Silvestre*.

Top Ten Names Beginning with S

GIRLS	BOYS
SOPHIE	SAMUEL
SUMMER	SEBASTIAN
SCARLETT	SAM
SOPHIA	SEAN
SIENNA	SIMON

Tabitha

This girl's name is of Hebrew origin meaning 'gazelle'. The fictional witch Tabitha Stephens, played by actress Elizabeth Montgomery (1933-95), was a fictional bearer of the name in the American TV sitcom *Bewitched* (1964-72).

Variant forms include: *Tabatha, Tabbie* and *Tabby*.

Talbot

This boy's name is of uncertain origin, possibly from Old French meaning 'cut bundle' or from obscure German roots. The name is associated with aristocracy, being the family name of the Earls of Shrewsbury.

Talia

This girl's name is of Hebrew and Aramaic origin and means 'lamb' or 'heaven's dew'. It could also be a shortened or pet form of *Natalia*.

Variant forms include: *Tahlia, Taliah* and *Talya*.

Tallullah

This girl's name is of Native American origin and means 'leaping water' taken from 'Tallulah Falls' in Georgia. The name may also come from the Gaelic name *Tallula*, meaning 'lady or princess'.

Variant forms include: *Talula* and *Tula*.

Tamara

This girl's name is of Hebrew origin, from 'tamar' meaning 'palm tree'. Tamara, in the Bible, was the name of Absalom's daughter who was renowned for her beauty, making the name a popular choice in the Christian world. It is often shortened to *Tam* or *Tammy*, which have both become independent names.

Variant forms include: *Tamarah* and *Tammi*.

Tamsin

The girl's name Tamsin is of English origin and is the Cornish variant of *Thomasina*, the feminine form of *Thomas*. The nickname *Tammy* is a popular shortened form.

Variant forms include: *Tamasine, Tamsine, Tamzen, Tamzin* and *Tasmin*.

Tansy

This girl's name is of Greek origin, from the plant name 'athanasia', a colourful yellow flower with a beautiful scent, meaning 'immortal'. Tansy first appeared as a name in the 1960s.

Tanya

This girl's name is of Russian origin, from the abbreviated form of the Latin 'Tatiana', which is from the house of Tatius. The name was taken up by English speakers in the early twentieth century.

Variant forms include: *Tania* and *Tonya*.

Tara

The girl's name is of Gaelic origin, and means 'hill' or 'star'. The name became very popular following the release of the iconic film *Gone with the Wind* (1939) in which Tara was the name of the fictional home of Scarlett O'Hara.

Variant forms include: *Tarah, Tarra* and *Tarrah*.

Tarquin

This boy's name is of Latin origin from the Roman family name of two Etruscan kings of pre-republican Rome in the fifth century BC. The name was popular in nineteenth-century poetry and drama.

Tatiana

This Russian girl's name, often shortened to *Tiana*, could be of Asian origin but could also be from the Roman family name Tatius, or from the Greek word 'tatto' meaning 'I arrange'.

Taylor

This unisex name is of English origin based on the surname given to people who were tailors. A famous bearer of the name was the poet Samuel Taylor Coleridge (1772-1834).

Tayler is a variant form.

Ted

The boy's name Ted is of English origin. The name is an abbreviated form of *Theodore*, a name of Greek origin meaning 'God's gift', or a shortened form of *Edward*, of Old English origin, meaning 'guardian of wealth'.

Variant form: *Teddy.*

Tegwen

The girl's name Tegwen is of Welsh origin from 'teg', which means 'pretty, fair', and 'gwen', which means 'white or blessed'. A popular variant form of the name is the English and Welsh *Tegan.*

Terence

This boy's name is of Latin origin from the family name of the Roman playwright Terence (Publius Terentius Afer, 195/185-159 BC). It is often shortened to *Terry*. Notable bearers of the name include the British actor Terence Stamp (b.1939).

Variant forms include: *Terance, Terrance, Terrence* and *Terrell*.

Teresa

The girl's name Teresa is of Greek origin, possibly from words meaning 'harvest' or 'guarding', or from the name of the Greek island of Therasia. The name is also spelt as *Theresa*. A famous bearer of the name is Mother Teresa (1910-97), who won the 1979 Nobel Peace Prize for her work in helping people in need across the world.

Variant forms include: *Terry* and *Tessa*.

Terry

This unisex name is of Old German origin meaning 'ruler of the tribe'. The name is also an abbreviated form of several other names including *Terence, Teresa* and *Theodore*.

Terri is a variant form.

Tess / Tessa

This girl's name is of Greek origin and is a shortened version of *Teresa*. It may also mean 'fifth child' or 'hunter and guardian'. *Tess of the d'Urbervilles* (1891) is a novel by Thomas Hardy.

Variant forms include: *Tessie, Tessy* and *Teza*.

Thalia

This girl's name is of Greek origin and means 'flourishing'. In Greek mythology Thalia, was one of the three Graces - goddesses who embodied beauty and art - and the muse of comedy.

Variant forms include: *Talia, Talie, Talley, Tally, Thaleia, Thalie* and *Thalya*.

Thelma

This girl's name is of Greek origin and means 'will, wish or volition'. The name was coined by British novelist Marie Corelli (1855-1924) for the Norwegian princess in her novel *Thelma* (1887). The 1991 American movie *Thelma* and *Louise* popularised the name.

Theo

The boy's name Theo is a variant of the Old German name *Theobald* and the Greek name *Theodore* and means 'brave people' or 'God's gift'.

Theodore

This boy's name is of Ancient Greek origin and means 'God's gift or gift of God'. The name was popular among early Christians and was borne by several saints. It is often shortened to *Theo*. American President Theodore Roosevelt (1858-1919) popularised the name and the teddy bear is named after him.

Variant forms include: *Ted, Teddie, Teddy* and *Theodor*.

Thomas

This enduringly popular boy's name is of Arabic origin and means 'twin'. It is often shortened to *Tom*. The name was borne by one of the twelve disciples, 'doubting Thomas', in the New Testament.

Variant forms include: *Thomson, Thompson, Tomlin, Tommie* and *Tommy*.

Thora

This girl's name is of Scandinavian origin and means 'Thor's goddess or struggle'. Thor was the Norse god of thunder. An uncommon name today, usage of the name peaked in the early twentieth century.

Tia

This girl's name is of Spanish origin and means 'aunt'. It is also a shortened form of the girl's name *Tiara*. In Latin the name may also mean 'joy and happiness'.

Top Ten Lucky Names

Names Rated Highly on the
'Lucky In Life Scale' by UK Psychologists.

GIRLS	BOYS
LUCY	JACK
KATY	RYAN
SOPHIE	PETER
LISA	DAVE
EMMA	JAMES

Tiara

This girl's name is of Latin origin and means 'headdress' and refers to the attractive jewelled crown worn by princesses and beauty queens and Her Majesty the Queen, as well as artistocrates and brides. Usage of the name peaked in the mid 1990s.

Variant forms include: *Tia* and *Tiarah*.

Tiffany

This girl's name is of Ancient Greek origin and means 'revelation or manifestation of God'. Today the name is also associated with the famous New York jeweller Tiffany & Co (established in 1837).

Variant forms include: *Tiffaney, Tiffani, Tiffanie, Tiffenie, Tiffeny, Tiffie, Tiffney, Tiffy, Tipheny, Tyffany* and *Tyffenie*.

Tiger

This boy's name is of English origin and refers to the 'tiger', an elegant wildcat predator. *Tigger* is a variant spelling of the name. American golfer Tiger Woods (b.1975) is a well-known bearer of the name, but he has recently had a much publicised fall from grace.

Tilly

The girl's name Tilly is a variant of the Old German names *Tilda* and *Matilda* and means 'one who is mighty or strong in battle'.

Variant forms include: *Tillie* and *Tally*.

Timothy

The boy's name Timothy is of Ancient Greek origin and means 'God's honour', 'honouring God' or 'honoured by God'. It is often shortened to *Tim*, which has become an independent name.

Variant forms include: *Timmy, Tymon* and *Tymothy*.

Tina

This girl's name is of Latin origin and a name ending, of names like *Christina, Katherina* and *Martina,* that has become a fairly popular independent name.

Variant forms include: *Teena, Tena, Tinamarie, Tine* and *Tiny.*

Toby

This unisex name, although it is more popular for boys, is of English origin and is a shortened form of the less current Hebrew name *Tobias,* which means 'God is good'.

Variant forms include: *Tobee, Tobey, Tobi* and *Tobie.*

Todd

This boy's name, and its variant spelling *Tod,* is of English origin and means 'fox', probably in reference to a 'fox hunter'.

Toddy and *Toddie* are unusual variants of the name.

Tom

This boy's name is a shortened version, which has become an independent name, of the Arabic *Thomas,* meaning 'twin'. American actors Tom Hanks (b.1956) and Tom Cruise (b.1962) are well-known bearers of this name.

Tommy is a variant form.

Tracy

This unisex name, although it tends to be more popular for girls, is of Irish and Gaelic origin and means 'warlike'. The name may also be derived from a place name in France meaning 'place of Thracius'.

Variant forms include: *Trace, Tracey, Traci* and *Tracie.*

Travis

The boy's name Travis, is of Old French origin and means 'to cross over'. The name derived from the job title for those who collected tolls from people passing over bridges or crossings.

Variant forms include: *Travers, Traviss* and *Travys.*

Trent

This boy's name is of Latin origin and means 'gushing waters'. It may also refer to the River Trent in England, or to someone who lived close to the river.

Variant forms include: *Trenten, Trentin* and *Trenton.*

Trevor

This boy's name is of Welsh origin and means 'the great settlement'. The name was first adopted by English speakers in the nineteenth century. The British actor Trevor Howard (1913–88) was a well-known bearer of the name.

Variant forms include: *Trevar* and *Trever.*

Trina

The girl's name Trina is probably based on the abbreviated form of names ending with -trina, for example, *Katrina,* but it is possibly also of Ancient Greek and Sanskrit origin meaning 'piercing'.

Variant forms include: *Treena, Trena* and *Trini.*

Tristan

This unisex name, although it is more common for boys, is of Celtic origin and means 'sad' and 'riot'. Tristan is the tragic hero in the medieval romance *Tristan and Isolde* and in Arthurian legend Tristan is a knight of the Round Table.

Variant forms include: *Tris, Tristam, Tristen, Tristin, Triston* and *Trystan.*

Troy

The boy's name Troy is of Irish and Gaelic origin and means 'foot soldier'. It may also mean 'man from Troyes', the Ancient Greek city where the Trojan wars were fought.

Trudy

The girl's name Trudy is a shortened form of the less commonly used Old German name *Gertrude,* which means 'strong or wholly beloved spear'. Trudy may also mean 'universal or immense'.

Variant forms include: *Trude, Trudey, Trudi* and *Trudie.*

Tucker

The boy's name Tucker is of Old English origin and means 'garment maker' or 'fuller'. It is often shortened to the nickname *Tuck*, which is also an independent name.

Tyler

This unisex name, although it tends to be more popular for boys, is of Old English origin and means 'worker in roof tiles'. The name is derived from the job title of someone who tiles roofs.

Variant forms: *Tilar, Ty, Tylar* and *Tylor*.

Tyrone

This boy's name is of Gaelic origin and means 'land of Eogam', meaning 'land of Owen'. It also refers to County Tyrone in Ireland. American film star Tyrone Power (1914-58) was a well-known bearer of the name.

Variant forms include: *Tirone, Ty, Tyron* and *Tyronne*.

Top Ten Names Beginning with T

GIRLS	BOYS
TIA	THOMAS
TILLY	TYLER
TAMSIN	TOBY
TARA	THEO
TERESA	TAYLOR

Ulrika

This girl's name, and its variant spelling *Ulrica*, is of Old German origin and means 'power of the home' or 'power of the wolf'. Other sources suggest it also means 'rich, powerful ruler'.

Uma

The unusual girl's name Uma is of Hindi and Sanskrit origin and means 'tumeric or flax'. American actress Uma Thurman (b.1970) is a well-known bearer of the name.

Una

This rare girl's name is of Ancient Greek, Latin and Celtic origin and means 'one'. Other sources suggest that it may also mean 'hunger' or 'lamb' or 'pure and chaste'.

Uri

This boy's name is of Hebrew origin and means 'my light', or 'my flame' or 'my God is light'. Israeli paranormal expert Uri Geller (b.1946) is a well-known bearer of the name.

Variant forms include: *Uriah* and *Yuri*.

Uriah

The boy's name Uriah is of Hebrew origin and means 'God is light'. The name was borne by several characters in the Bible, but the use of the name declined dramatically when it became associated with the cringe-making and bootlicking character Uriah Heep in Charles Dickens' novel *David Copperfield* (1850).

Variant forms include: *Uri* and *Yuri*.

Ursula

This girl's name is of Scandinavian and Latin origin and means 'little female bear'. The name was borne by legendary fourth-century Saint Ursula, who led a pilgrimage of 11,000 handmaidens against the Huns.

Variant forms include: *Ursa, Ursala, Ursulina, Ursuline* and *Urszula*.

Val

This unisex name, although it tends to be more popular for boys, is of Latin origin and is a shortened version of the unisex name *Valentine* and female name *Valerie*. It means 'healthy and strong'.

Valerie

This girl's name, which is often shortened to *Val*, is of Latin origin and means 'healthy and strong'. The name shot to prominence with the cover of the song 'Valerie' (2007) by English singer-songwriter Amy Winehouse (b.1983).

Variant forms include: *Valaree, Valarie, Valery, Vallerie, Vallery, Vallie, Vallorey, Vallorie, Vallory* and *Valorie*.

Top Ten Names After Artists

GIRLS	BOYS
MARY	VINCENT
GEORGIA	MARC
EMILY	ANDY
LOUISE	JACKSON
ELISABETH	PAUL

Vanessa

This girl's name is of English origin and was coined in the early eighteenth century by the Irish poet Jonathan Swift (1667-1745). American actress Vanessa Anne Hudgens (b.1988) is a well-known bearer of the name.

Variant forms include: *Vanesa, Vanesse, Vannessa, Venesa* and *Venessa*.

Vaughn

This boy's name is of Welsh origin and means 'little one'. Although its use was widespread in the past, with its usage peaking in 1949, the name has since experienced a decline in popularity.

Vaughan is a variant form.

Venus

This girl's name is of Latin origin. In Roman mythology Venus is the goddess of love and beauty. American tennis player Venus Williams (b.1980) is a well-known bearer of the name.

Vera

This girl's name is of Slavic and Latin origin and means 'faith and truth'. The name is familiar to many due to the British singer Dame Vera Lynn (b.1917), the forces' sweetheart during World War II.

Variant forms include: *Veera* and *Veira*.

Verity

The girl's name Verity is of Latin origin and means 'virtue and truth'. Along with names such as *Constance, Prudence, Chastity* and *Hope*, it was a Puritan virtue name.

Verna

The girl's name Verna is of Latin origin and means 'spring green' and 'true'. Used since the early twentieth century, it may also be the feminine form of *Vernon*.

Variant forms include: *Verda, Verne, Verneta* and *Virna*.

Vernon

The uncommon boy's name Vernon is of Old French origin and probably derives from a place name and aristocratic surname meaning 'alder grove' or 'place of flourishing alders'.

Variant forms include: *Lavern, Vern* and *Verne.*

Verona

This girl's name is of Latin origin and a variant of *Veronica*. It may also derive from the place name of an Italian city that is a popular tourist destination.

Veronica

This girl's name is of Latin origin and means 'bearer of victory' and 'true image'. Saint Veronica was a pious woman said to have offered Christ a cloth to wipe his face as he carried the cross. According to legend, an image of his face was left on the cloth.

Variant forms include: *Vera, Vernice* and *Verona.*

Victor

This boy's name is of Latin origin and means 'champion and conqueror'. Sometimes shortened to *Vic*, it is a very popular saint's name and the masculine form of *Victoria*.

Victoria

This enduringly popular girl's name is of Latin origin and means 'victor'. It is the name of the Roman goddess of victory. The name has strong royal associations for many due to Britain's Queen Victoria (1819-1901). It is often shortened to far less formal names, such as *Vic* and *Vicky*.

Variant forms include: *Tori, Toria, Torie, Tory, Vicci, Vickee, Vickey, Vici* and *Vicki*.

Vincent

The boy's name Vincent is of Latin origin and means 'winning and conquering'. It is often shortened to *Vince, Vinnie* or *Vinny*, which have all become fairly popular independent names.

Violet

This girl's name, and the variant spelling *Viola*, is of Latin origin and means 'the colour purple'. First used in the early nineteenth century, it was one of the earliest flower names.

Virgil

This uncommon boy's name is of Latin origin and means 'staff bearer'. The name is familiar to some through the writings of Virgil (Publius Vergilius Maro), the Roman poet and philosopher in the first century BC.

Virginia

This girl's name is of Latin origin with the meaning 'virgin and maiden'. The name is popular in America. The first child born in the Americas to English parents, in 1587, was named Virginia Dare.

Variant forms include: *Geena, Gina, Ginny, Ginya, Jinny, Virgina* and *Virginnia*.

Vivian

This popular unisex name, although it is far more common for girls, is of Latin origin and means 'alive and lively'. The name is sometimes shortened to *Viv*.

Variant forms include: *Viviane, Vivianne, Vivien, Vivienne* and *Vivyan*.

Top Ten Names Beginning with U & V

GIRLS	BOYS
VICTORIA	VICTOR
UMA	VINCENT
VANESSA	VAL
VALERIE	VAUGHAN
VIVIAN	VERNON

Wade

This boy's name is of Old English and Scandinavian origin and is from an Old English surname which means 'river ford' or 'one who dwells by the river ford'.

Variant forms include: *Wayde* and *Waydell*.

Wallace

This boy's name is of Old French origin and means 'from Wales'. It was originally a Scottish surname, which refers to foreigners from the south, and became a first name in honour of the Scottish patriot Sir William Wallace (1272/3-1305), who was executed by the English while fighting for his country's independence.

Variant forms include: *Wallas, Wallie, Wallis* and *Wally*.

Walter

This boy's name is of Old German origin and means 'to rule' or 'commander of the army'. It is often shortened to *Walt*. American cartoonist Walt Disney (1901-66) was a famous bearer of the name.

Wanda

This girl's name is of Slavic origin and means 'tribe of the vandals', in reference to an ancient Slavic tribe who may have inspired the term 'vandalism'. Wanda may also mean 'wanderer' in Old German.

Variant forms include: *Wandah, Wendy, Wonda* and *Wonnda*.

Warren

This boy's name is of Old English origin and means 'game park', or 'watchman'. It may also be from Old French, meaning 'stockyard'. American actor Warren Beatty (b.1937) is a famous bearer of the name.

Wayne

This popular boy's name is of Old English origin and means 'driver' or 'wagon builder'. English footballer Wayne Rooney (b.1985) is a well-known bearer of the name.

Variant forms include: *Wain, Waine* and *Wayn*.

Wendell

This boy's name is of Old German origin and means 'wanderer'. The popularity of the name peaked in the 1940s, but has subsequently fallen and is infrequently used today.

Variant forms include: *Wendale, Wendall* and *Wendel*.

Wendy

This enduringly popular girl's name is of English origin and means 'friend'. In Welsh the meaning may be 'white circle and moon', and in Old German it may be 'wanderer'. The name is familiar to many as the name of the fictional character in *Peter Pan*, J. M. Barrie's classic children's play (1904) and story (1911).

Variant forms include: *Wenda, Wendee, Wendi, Wendie* and *Windy*.

Wesley

This boy's name is of Old German origin and means 'west meadow'. It is often shortened to *Wes*. American actor Wesley Snipes (b.1962) is a well-known bearer of the name, although he has recently fallen from grace.

Variant forms include: *Wesly, Wessley, Westleigh* and *Westley*.

Whitney

This girl's name is of Old English origin and means 'white meadow'. Originally a boy's name, it became popular for girls in the 1980s due to American singer Whitney Houston (b.1963).

Variant forms include: *Whiteney, Whitnea, Whitnee, Whitny, Whittney* and *Whittnie*.

Wilfred

This boy's name is of Old English origin and means 'desiring peace'. It is often shortened to *Will*. The name was borne by Saint Wilfrid (*c.*633–*c.*709), an English bishop at the Council of Whitby.

Variant forms include: *Wilfrid, Willfred* and *Willfryd*.

Willamina

This unusual girl's name is a variant of the German girl's name *Wilhelmina*, which means 'will and desire', as well as 'helmet, protection'. It is currently not popular as a girl's name.

William

This boy's name is of German origin and means 'will, desire, determined and resolute'. The name became very popular after the 1066 Norman Conquest by William the Conqueror (*c.*1028–87), the first Norman King of England. It was the name of British playwright William Shakespeare (1564–1616), and the firstborn son of the current Prince of Wales is Prince William (b.1982).

Variant forms include: *Bill, Billy, Will, Willie, Wills, Willson, Willy, Wilmer, Wilmot, Wilmott, Wilson* and *Wim*.

Willow

The girl's name Willow is of English origin and refers to the pliant, slender tree called a willow. It is a fairly recent name that is currently growing in popularity.

Winifred

This girl's name is of Welsh and Old English origin and means 'blessed, joy and friend of peace' and 'reconciled'. The name was borne by Saint Winifred, a seventh-century Welsh princess.

Variant forms include: *Winne, Winnie, Winnifred, Wynafred, Wynifred, Wynn, Wynne* and *Wynnifred*.

Winona

This girl's name is of Native American origin and means 'firstborn daughter'. American actress Winona Ryder (b.1971) has made the name familiar in recent times.

Variant forms include: *Winnie, Winnona, Winonna, Wynona* and *Wynonna*.

Winston

This boy's name is of Old English origin and means 'stone', 'settlement', 'friend' and 'joyful'. British Prime Minister Sir Winston Spencer-Churchill (1874-1965) was a famous bearer of the name.

Variant forms include: *Win, Winn, Winsten, Winstonn, Wynstan* and *Wynston*.

Woody

This boy's name is a variant of the rarely used English name *Woodrow*, which has become a more popular name in its own right. It means 'he who lives by a wood'.

Top Ten Names After Royalty

GIRLS	BOYS
ELIZABETH	CHARLES
VICTORIA	WILLIAM
ISABELLA	JAMES
ALEXANDRA	LOUIS
ANNE	HENRY

Wyatt

The boy's name Wyatt is of Old English origin and means 'war' and 'strength'. The name was borne by well-known American gunfighter and lawman Wyatt Earp (1848-1929).

Variant forms include: *Wiatt, Wye* and *Wyeth*.

Wynn

This uncommon unisex name is of Old English origin and means 'fair, blessed and holy' and 'friend of peace'. It is also a shortened form of the girl's name *Winifred*.

Variant forms include: *Win, Winn, Wyn, Wyndell, Wynne* and *Wynton*.

Top Ten Names after Authors

GIRLS	BOYS
JOANNE	CHARLES
CHARLOTTE	WILLIAM
EMILY	MARK
JANE	DAN
STEPHANIE	IAN

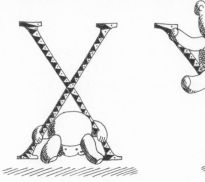

Xander

The boy's name Xander, which is a shortened form of the Greek boy's name *Alexander*, has become a modestly popular independent name. It means 'defender or protector of men'.

Xandra

The uncommon girl's name Xandra, and its variant spellings *Xandria* and *Xandra*, is a variant of the Greek girl's name *Alexandra*, which means 'protector or defender of men'.

Xavier

This boy's name is of Spanish, Basque and Arabic origin and means 'bright and brilliant new home'. Most used by Roman Catholics, the fictional Professor Xavier of *The X-Men* comics (1963-present) and *X-Men* film series (2000-present), has made the name more familiar.

Variant forms include: *Xever* and *Zavier*.

Xena

This girl's name is of Ancient Greek origin and means 'stranger' and 'hospitable'. *Xena: Warrior Princess* was a popular supernatural fantasy adventure American TV series (1995-2001).

Zena is a variant form.

Top Ten Names Associated with Animals

GIRLS	BOYS
CAT	TIGER
ROBIN	JAY
FAWN	JOEY
KITTY	PHOENIX
EVE	BILLY

Xuxa

The unusual girl's name Xuxa (pronounced ZHOO-SHA) is of Latin origin and a nickname for the Hebrew name *Susan*, meaning 'lily', which has become an independent name.

Yasmine

The girl's name Yasmine, and its variant spelling *Yasmin*, is a less popular variant of the popular Old French and Persian name *Jasmine*, which means 'jasmine' or 'jasmine flower'.

Yolanda

This girl's name is of debated Greek, Germanic and Spanish origin and means 'violet flower'. It is a variant of *Yolande*, which in turn is the French variant of the name *Violet*.

Variant forms include: *Iolanda, Yollande, Yolantha, Yolanthe* and *Yulanda*.

Yves

This boy's name is of German and French origin and means 'yew'. A saint's name, it has become familiar in recent times due to the French fashion designer Yves Saint Laurent (1936-2008).

Variant forms include: *Ivo* and *Yvon*.

Yvette

The girl's name Yvette is of German and French origin and means 'yew'. It is a variant of *Yvonne*. The usage of the name peaked in the late 1960s and it just remains in modest use today.

Yvonne

This girl's name is of French and German origin and means 'yew'. It is the feminine form of *Yves*. It may once have been an archer's occupational name as yew was used to make bows.

Variant forms include: *Evonne, Ivonne, Yevette, Yvetta, Yvette, Yvone* and *Yvonna*.

Zachary

The boy's name Zachary, a variant of the less commonly used ancient Hebrew names *Zechariah* and *Zachery*, means 'the Lord God has remembered or recalled'.

Zaharah

This girl's name, and its variant spellings *Zahara* and *Zahra*, is of Arabic and Hebrew origin and means 'shining, apparent, bright and flowering'. The name is infrequently used today.

Zak

This boy's name, and its variant spellings *Zac, Zach* and *Zack*, is itself a variant of the Hebrew names *Isaac*, which means 'to laugh' and 'laughter' and *Zachery*, which means 'the Lord has remembered'. In recent times the name has been steadily growing in popularity.

Zara

This girl's name is of Arabic origin and means 'blossoming flower' and 'radiance'. It may also be a variant form of *Sarah*. Rarely used until the mid-twentieth century, in a departure from British royalty naming conventions, it was chosen by Princess Anne (b.1950) and Mark Phillips (b.1948) for their daughter Zara Phillips (b.1981).

Variant forms include: *Zarah, Zaria* and *Zayra*.

Zeb

This boy's name is a variant form, which has become an independent name of the far less commonly used ancient Hebrew names *Zebediah, Zebedee* and *Zebulon*, meaning 'gift of God' and 'place of honour'.

Zelda

The girl's name Zelda is a pet name for *Griselda*, which is of Old German origin meaning 'dark battle'. The variant name *Zelde* is of Yiddish origin meaning 'happiness'.

Zeno

This boy's name is of Ancient Greek origin and means 'gift or life of Zeus'. Zeus was the leader of the Olympian gods and goddesses. *Zena* is probably the feminine form.

Variant forms include: *Zenon* and *Zino*.

Zeus

The boy's name Zeus is of Ancient Greek origin and means 'living, light and deity'. It was the name of the leader of the Olympian gods and father of many other gods and goddesses.

Zia

This girl's name, and its variant spelling *Zea*, is of Arabic, Hebrew and Latin origin and means 'bright, glowing and splendid' and 'to tremble'. In Italian it also means 'aunt'.

Zoe

The popular girl's name Zoe is of Ancient Greek origin and means 'life'. It was adopted by English speakers in the nineteenth century following the 1845 Geraldine Jewsbury novel, *Zoe, A History of Two Lives*.

Variant forms include: *Zoee, Zoey* and *Zoie*.

Top Ten Names
Beginning with W, X, Y & Z

GIRLS	BOYS
ZARA	WILLIAM
ZOE	ZAK
WHITNEY	WARREN
YVONNE	WESLEY
WENDY	WAYNE